CW00516532

HEAR ME EVOLVE

HEAR ME EVOLVE

Voices of the collective

EL JEDRAS & SARAH ELLIS

First Published in 2023 by El Jedras and Sarah Ellis

Copyright © 2023 El Jedras - Evolveology

The right of El Jedras and Sarah Ellis to be identified
as the author of this Work has been asserted by them in
accordance with sections 77 and 78 of the Copyright, Designs
and Patents Act 1988

All rights reserved. No part of this publication may be
reproduced, stored in a retrieval system, copied in any form
or by any means, electronic, mechanical, photocopying,
recording or otherwise transmitted without written
permission from the author.

Typesetting by Laura B Empowered Words
www.laurab-empoweredwords.com

INTRODUCTION

Welcome to "Hear Me Evolve: Voices of the Collective." As you hold this book in your hands, and begin to turn each page, you're opening your heart to the diverse, resilient and soul baring voices of women.

This anthology was born from a shared journey—a summit that brought together 21 authors to shed light on stories of healing, growth, and transformation. As you read through these pages, you'll embark on a journey that transcends individual experiences, joining an ensemble of voices that resonate with the human spirit's capacity to endure, learn, and evolve.

With each chapter, an author steps forward to offer a piece of their unique journey, a glimpse into their challenges, their victories, and the wisdom they've gathered along the way. From navigating the depths of adversity to embracing the light of hope, these stories form a tapestry of resilience, woven with threads of empathy, authenticity, and shared purpose.

But this anthology is more than a collection of narratives; it's a catalyst for change. With every page turned, you contribute to our mission to raise awareness for mental health and support a cause close to our hearts. The proceeds from sale of this book will reach out to "Hopefull Handbags," extending our collective embrace to survivors of domestic abuse, guiding them towards a life of strength and boundless possibilities.

We are a collective of divine souls on a path to deeper learning, growth, and healing—our voices determined to uplift and empower. "Hear Me Evolve: Voices of the Collective" invites you to connect, reflect, and emerge with a renewed sense of purpose—a purpose that echoes the words of every author within.

Thank you for joining us on this transformative journey, for giving life to these voices, and for embracing the power of evolution, healing, and hope.

Together we can evolve.

With love & gratitude,

El and Sarah

Disclaimer

In the pages that follow, we, a group of courageous women, share unfiltered and raw stories encompassing experiences of abuse, trauma, and the transformative journey to healing. These narratives are deeply personal, occasionally containing explicit language and descriptions. Our goal is to provide an authentic and unvarnished portrayal of our lives, shining a light on the often silenced and misunderstood aspects of our lives. While our intention is to raise awareness and offer support to those who have faced similar challenges, we acknowledge that certain stories may be triggering or uncomfortable for some readers. We encourage you to approach this book with mindfulness and self-awareness. If you find certain content overwhelming, we recommend taking breaks or seeking support. Our collective hope is that through these stories, we can foster understanding, empathy, and a profound sense of unity among those who have walked similar paths. May our stories kindle the spark of empowerment, propelling individuals to embark on their own quests for happiness and healing.

CONTENTS

YOU ARE AN EVOLVING MASTERPIECE
EL JEDRAS   3

SELF-LOVE ISN'T SELFISH, IT'S A NECESSITY
COLETTE MALCOLM   13

CHANGE YOUR STORY CHANGE YOUR LIFE
TRACEY PAYNE   23

YOU ARE STRONGER THAN YOU GIVE YOURSELF
CREDIT FOR
LOUISE FLETCHER   33

AN EMPOWERED EMPATH
LISA WILLIAMS   43

FINDING MY VOICE
JANINE MCDONALD   53

SHAME, GUILT, AND GASLIGHTING, 'YOU KNOW IT'S
ALL YOUR FAULT!'
MICHELLE LOUISE SMITH   63

UNLEASHING YOUR POTENTIAL: CONNECTING,
COMMUNICATING, AND IGNITING CHANGE FROM
WITHIN!
    HAYLEY SU BUCHANAN   73

RISE FROM THE ASHES INTO YOUR IMPERFECT
MASTERPIECE
    KELISHA TAYLOR   83

BE YOU
    KERI DENNEY   91

REVELATIONS OF A BETRAYED HEART
    NIKKI PINTO   101

RECLAMATION
    CHRISTINE KENNY   111

FROM ADDICTION TO EMPOWERMENT
    SARAH IBRAHIM   121

WHO'S THAT GIRL
    NAOMI SHEPHERD   131

RISE OF THE FEMININE
    CHERYL BECKWORTH   141

A GODDESS CAN BE DESTROYED (BUT ONLY FOR ONE
MORE DAY)
    NIXIE FOSTER   151

OFF THE ROLLERCOASTER INTO MY LOWER TOX LANE
    AISLING LOUISE OWENS NASH   161

FROM BROKEN WINGS TO A BEAUTIFUL BUTTERFLY
SHARON ELAINE HODGKINSON   171

DANCING WITH DESPERATION: A TALE OF DARING TO
BE DIFFERENT
RACHEL JENNINGS COUDRON   181

IS THAT ALL THERE IS? PERSPECTIVE AND INCREASING
GRATITUDE
JACKIE McGLOUGHLIN   191

YOU ARE GOOD ENOUGH, I AM GOOD ENOUGH
SARAH ELLIS   201

EPILOGUE   210

YOU ARE AN EVOLVING MASTERPIECE

El Jedras

The person writing this chapter is not the same individual from 5 years ago. This book was inspired by my own journey, a journey that echoes with countless others. It unravels the tale of the 'good girl,' tirelessly seeking to please everyone and fit into various circles at home, with family, friends, colleagues, and anyone within reach. We often find ourselves forced into silence, moulded by those who innocently envisioned the person we were meant to be. Suppressing our voices, rationalising abuse, and conforming to the societal standards imposed upon women as they mature. The longing to belong, to gain acceptance, to be desired and cherished, all while losing ourselves to an identity we never got to choose.

I wanted so badly to be that good girl, I really did, I wanted to be everything that they wanted me to be. The only problem was, no matter how hard I tried to mould myself into what they envisioned I just didn't feel like I fit.

3

I wanted to be a good girl, upholding the rules and traditions of our Muslim family. However, this path wasn't always smooth. An inexplicable internal stir pushed me to challenge a few norms, to voice thoughts when silence was expected. I wrestled with the perception of a "good girl" staying mute, as I longed to explore many things that were deemed off-limits especially for a girl, particularly in our culture. In the midst of childhood innocence, telling right from wrong wasn't always easy. Wasn't it all just child's play? What did being a good girl really look like?

Looking back, I wish my young self comprehended what I now do. That being a "good" girl shouldn't have meant blindly giving myself to every demand. Those hidden secrets within me, like deep, dark holes, bearing their own weight. I wish I foresaw the lasting repercussions of the games I played; the damage embedded in the innocence that was me. Childhood memories now tainted by the pursuits of goodness; those moments where yes seemed the right option. It's these memories that I tried to forget, I tried to make myself believe it wasn't wrong, that perhaps I was misreading all the times he created games to be close to me, to be alone with me. The intimate moments created in a concept I only recognised as play for so very long. I was too young to understand when it all first started, and a teenager by the time I understood that I could in fact say no and that I did in fact have a choice realising that this was no longer innocent child play. The magnitude of what I was allowing hit hard. I was drowning in the flashbacks and confusion, guilt and shame stirred together within me creating a cocktail of emotions I wasn't ready to digest. I was awakened before my time and was confused by the stirring feeling of wanting to explore my body for me yet seeing it as a gift to others. It took me a long time to understand that my body is my gift and no one else's.

I wanted so badly to be good, and to follow what was expected of me, I tried. I really did.

In school I wanted to fit in, I wanted to just blend in and be friends with everyone and be seen as one of the crowd but I somehow didn't. I didn't feel like one of them, I felt like one of me, just me, like I didn't fit in. I tried to dress like others and talk like others, tried to blend in by straightening my very dark Mediterranean curly frizzy hair. I tried the odd fashion accessory; I mean who didn't have a pair of kickers or Chelsea boots right? But yet I still felt weird somehow, like it was me and then all of them. The one thing I did have was my body and my sexuality and I already understood the power of this, this seemed like the easiest way to get the attention I needed and to fit in, so I thought. I look back and see the situations I allowed myself to get into, the amount of trust I put in the hands of men. I started to see that men couldn't always be trusted and even those you thought loved you could hurt you in the most intimate ways. My secret childhood 'games' were finally over but I soon learnt that kid's games could turn into adult games and that my body could still be the choice of others and not myself. My body was still my power even after that one night but yet my trust was lost in that room with a man I thought I may marry one day. I was now learning about love and trust in a new light.

I wanted so badly to be good, and to follow what was expected of me, to feel like I fit it, and trust everyone, especially my family. I tried; I really did.

When I went off to university, I thought this would be my break, this would be my chance at freedom, to explore, to grow into my own identity. But it wasn't as easy as I thought it would be, I suddenly became the opposite of so many traits I thought I wasn't. I was so sensible it was actually ridiculous; I couldn't relax and do what University students are meant to do. Wild parties were too wild, I certainly could not drink like others too. So here I was the good girl in mind, but my body certainly wanted to explore, but of course my mind kept that from happening, I mean can you think of the shame?

It took me a while to figure it out but by that time I had, I had fallen into my second serious relationship. Everything was moving super-fast and I was falling into the path that I was born into, yet not the one I really wanted but what I had downloaded as my identity. The sensible young lady, who was respectful and kind, and a wife and a mother, that was the expectation, and it ran through me like my own blood.

I wanted so badly to be good, and to follow what was expected of me, to feel like I fit it, and trust everyone especially my family, and never do something that could bring me or my family shame, I tried I really did.

It was at that moment I applied the brakes in my relationship, I wanted to have fun, I wanted to play and explore and find myself. I wanted to see what the other side of a good girl really was. I wanted to evolve into something new and exciting, little did I know that this would take me into a dark and toxic relationship where the sensible was replaced with excitement, but also drugs, rejection and abuse and wounds that would forever need healing.

Whilst hiding my toxic relationship my career began to grow, I lived for my career as it was everything I thought I needed and wanted. I was very much living the dream to the outside world. How does it go again? A great job, a fiancé, a home, and a cat of course, I mean it was looking pretty much on track for becoming a wife and a stay at home mother, except this was the story created by others. I was living the generational dream but in reality, in my personal reality it was not the love and happiness and success I had dreamed of.

At work I did everything to be a success and to fit in with my peers. I was the yes girl and I mean I suppose it worked. I got to tick off a lot of promotions, pay rises and job offers but I also still never found my own true identity and I was an adult now. I was just living as the identity of a girl that was created by everyone else, all the different parts of me built piece by piece by everyone and everything I had learnt until this point. Was that correct? Was that actually who I was meant to be? What did everyone else expect of me? It didn't feel right to me, I felt there was more to be, to create, and to become.

I wanted so badly to be good, and to follow what was expected of me, to feel like I fit it, and trust everyone especially my family, and never do something that could bring me or my family shame, and of course be successful in my career, I tried, I really did.

After 8 long years, that relationship finally came to an end. I ceased the battle of desperately seeking love, even when it meant enduring toxic lies which washed away making me stay year after year. It was the kind of love that was rotting so deeply on the inside but hidden from the outside world. I found myself addicted to the hope of improvement, wanting him to change, wanting him to give up the toxic habits and to desire me more than his destructive habits. I wanted him to desire me the way I thought he would when we first met and he lured me in with his words and scent. I wished this love to be real but soon the rotten core began to spread to the surface too and every attempt to leave failed until one day.

I broke free, I ran away, told lies, and cheated, all in pursuit of my freedom. I wanted to embrace the girl I truly was, the good girl with a fun and adventurous spirit. The girl who could be sensible and mature, yet also had a wild free and spiritual side waiting to break free. I longed to be loved as if I were the sole focus of my partner's world. Craving a passion so intense, it would saturate my very being, soaking me to the core. I yearned to be wanted so deeply that a single glance would bind us in an unbreakable nourishing hold. To feel a sense of security I had never known before—to be myself, to be heard, to breathe, to play, to explore, and to evolve into the person I was always meant to be... Me.

I wanted so badly to be good, and to follow what was expected of me, to feel like I fit it, and trust everyone especially my family, and never do something that could bring me or my family shame, and of course be successful in my career, and become the wife and mother my parents expected me to be, I tried, I really did.

But this wasn't really what I wanted, not really. I badly wanted to be free to decide my own future vision. I no longer wanted to live under someone's vision.

Since then, the past 15 years have been dedicated to rebuilding my identity, discovering my true self, and shedding the layers of what everyone else expected of me. Pulling myself apart to uncover and reveal the layers underneath that were hidden, healing from the past I had stored away. I crafted new belief systems that aligned with my own values, granting myself the power to forgive in order to move on. I created space to re-learn how to love myself and my body correctly, so I can show others how I truly wanted to be loved. Throughout this journey, the questions echoed within: Who am I? Who do I aspire to be? How can I authentically present myself? What are my genuine desires?

You enter the world with a predefined identity – your

name, your parents' religion, and more, all bestowed upon you. It's a straightforward, beautiful gift, naturally embraced and absorbed. This, I labelled as our "identity blueprint," much like constructing a house. Just as a house's plans are drawn and blueprints approved before building commences, similarly, we're born with a name, an identity, and a vision of our future as adults, all envisioned by our family and loved ones.

The truth is, whenever we desire to alter something within our identity blueprint, we face challenges. It might be as simple as changing our hair colour, using our voice to express our true feelings, or breaking down a relationship. Yet, no matter how big or small the change, it can feel daunting, frightening, and difficult for both us and those who designed the original blueprint. More often than not, they remain unaware of the profound impact they have bestowed upon us with their expectations and beliefs.

Since the moment of our first breath, our lives have been steered by the well-intentioned visions of family and loved ones, predetermining our future before we even have a say. This path becomes ingrained in our subconscious, making it difficult to welcome change, leaving us feeling uneasy. I once conducted an experiment during a large group session, asking them to alter their morning routine by making their usual hot beverage in a different order, for example those who would add water first perhaps could add milk first. The next morning the response flooded my phone with messages of discomfort and challenge, all for a simple cup of tea. Habits form not only in our actions but also in our thoughts and beliefs. The more we repeat, the deeper they become imprinted within us, making change seem daunting, even when it's just a cup of tea.

We evolve into this blueprint as it becomes our narrative, often without contemplating who we truly aspire to be. Five years ago, I grappled with my identity, battling anxiety and social apprehension. I hid away from photos and videos, and any I did take, even alongside my partner, I'd delete later. My confidence had escaped me, and decision-making felt draining and intense. But that girl no longer defines me; I have evolved and take pride in the journey I've undertaken.

My reawakening was extraordinary; it's challenging to articulate the transformative shifts I've undergone. Finally, I'm liberated from the weight of others' expectations and pressures to conform. My intuitive psychic abilities guide me, supporting my journey and empowering others in their own profound transformations. Coupled with becoming a mindset coach for women and exploring a range of modalities to enhance my own growth and healing I knew it was time to share what I had with the world, and I am so glad I did.

In 2020, I founded Evolveology®, a space for women to explore, heal, and evolve into their genuine and soulful identities. I'm a visionary leader with a passion that thrives on helping others shape lives they've intentionally designed. My biggest teaching, to trust yourself! Trusting yourself and the decisions you make was one of the hardest things I did. Pushing aside my constant procrastination and fears, just fully trusting myself to make the moves I needed to be free of a life that was not serving my true identify or my happiness.

My own path is ever evolving, and I am proud, navigating a life I wholeheartedly recognise, one I've built through intentional choices. A 15-year marriage crafted with love, passion, and safety, and everything in between, all the things I desired for so long, alongside becoming a mum, a SEN mum to my three little heroes. Please know you can have it all, everything you desire you don't need to choose between your happiness and success or love you can choose right now to have them all. This was one of the best decisions I ever made. So let this be a reminder to all who read it—that within you lies the strength to be all that you wish to be and have all you wish to dream of, unburdened by the constraints of others' expectations. Your identity is not fixed; we are forever evolving, you are a canvas in progress, a beautiful evolution of your true self. Embrace it with love, courage, and unwavering authenticity.

You have the power to shape your identity, to break free from the blueprint and craft a unique masterpiece that reflects the vibrant colours of your soul regardless of your past or current experiences. Embrace the journey of self-discovery, where you will uncover the hues that make you uniquely you.

Together we can evolve.

**

El Jedras is a visionary leader, CEO of Evolveology® and Feminology UK Retreats. As an Intuitive Psychic and mindset coach, El guides transformative journeys for personal and business growth. A compassionate advocate for mental health awareness, she supports Hopefull Handbags, helping survivors of domestic abuse. El is a two-time best-selling author and a proud SEN mum of three little heroes. Her passion lies in empowering others to embrace their power and find success and happiness. Join her on a journey of evolution and inspiration @eljedras

SELF-LOVE ISN'T SELFISH, IT'S A NECESSITY

Colette Malcolm

Who I am today is a very a different person to who I was several years ago and that's because I've been on one hell of a journey of self-discovery and self-love. I will pre-warn you now that there are talks of suicidal thoughts and self-harm within this chapter. But I am a big believer in sharing my story so that others do not have to go through it or think they are alone. So often we don't talk about mental health issues because we are too ashamed or don't want to burden people around us, but it shouldn't be that way. I was that person that kept it all in and as you will read, that wasn't the best idea. So now, I will always keep on talking about my story and if it helps just one person, that makes me happy.

Little did I know that my childhood would go on to have such an impact on the way I felt about myself. Growing up with one parent who battled with alcohol issues and the other parent, even though they were around sometimes, it often felt like they weren't. I'm not saying I had a terrible childhood, but it wasn't the best. I didn't go without though, but if I am honest looking back on it, I now see that I was showered with more presents than presence. Something I think a lot of people will be able to relate to. Even if they don't want to admit it. It's easy for people to replace love for things.

I had to grow up fast and looking back I didn't really have anyone to show me the way. I was too busy looking after others. A pattern that repeated itself throughout my life. My first proper relationship ended up being psychologically abusive. He ended up going through depression himself and even though he treated me badly, I still wanted to take care of him. Well, until it got too much. I stayed for as long as I did as honestly, I didn't value myself enough, nor did I fully understand what was going on. That and the fact I was told repeatedly I was too fat and ugly and that no one else would ever want me. Something that stuck with me for a very long time. Thankfully that relationship did end. But it wasn't all roses after that.

My own relationship with alcohol was not great. I started drinking from a young age. Like a lot of people my age, drinking over at the park on the weekend was the highlight of the week. We used to hang around outside the shops and get whoever we could to buy us the cheapest and strongest alcohol we could get our hands on. Most of the time we didn't even enjoy the taste, but if it got us drunk, that was ok. Never knowing when to stop and often putting myself in dangerous situations was sadly the norm though. But despite all of that I somehow managed to bumble through life. Holding down good jobs and seemingly looking ok to the outside world. However, on the inside I was unhappy. I look back at the old pictures of me and I can tell she wasn't happy. I can tell her smile was fake. It makes me just want to go back and give her a big hug.

I threw myself into exercise and controlling my diet in a way that I now see was unhealthy. At the time though, if anyone challenged my 4am crazy exercise starts or tiny portions of food I was eating, I would argue that they weren't motivated. I would also spout a whole load of fitness motivational quotes all over social media. I cringe when my Facebook memories pop up to be honest now. But I didn't know at the time that ultimately what I was doing was trying to hold on to some element of control in my life. Even when I lost a tonne of weight, I wasn't truly happy, so that proves to me now that weight loss was never the goal.

The goal was finding myself. But I didn't know at the time. I had nothing to compare my feelings with, so I was just doing what I thought was best. This was working ok up until when I went through my divorce and then bam! Depression and anxiety hit me like a steam train. You can only push something down for so long before it is inevitably going to bubble up and explode. I went to the doctors and was prescribed antidepressants. Something I was reluctant to take at first, but I felt at this point I had no choice as I didn't feel right at all. I was also put on the waiting list for counselling. After my initial phone consultation, I was told it would be 3-4 months before I could be seen. Not what you want to hear when you just need the help right there and then.

My moods ended up erratic, I drank even more, which is insane considering alcohol is a depressant. Again, something I didn't know at the time. I ended up self-harming by cutting myself and sometimes even burning my arms with a lighter. I still have the scars now and I doubt the bad ones will ever go. I didn't think about that at the time. I just wanted a release. Then on the really bad days I had suicidal thoughts. To the point it was planned out. I feel upset now thinking about how low I actually got. I remember one day lying in bed, looking up at the ceiling and thinking I saw the shadow of a black dog up there.

It was at this point I had a strong feeling that I needed to do something. I thought to myself I either get help right now or I will no longer be here. It sounds extreme, but it was true. Makes me feel sad just writing that, but that was how it was. I called the counselling emergency number and if I'm honest I don't remember what was said, but I know within 2 days I was seen by a counsellor. We had 4 sessions scheduled, which really isn't a lot when you are in a bad place, but I guess it was better than nothing at all.

During these sessions, we briefly covered some of the childhood issues that had affected me, and it did help to put some of the things to bed. The suicidal thoughts thankfully ended up going, but my anxiety was still there, along with a feeling that I just wasn't myself. It wasn't until I started working with a holistic mindset coach that I realised what the missing piece was. That piece was self-love. I had none. I had no self-respect. No boundaries with anyone. No self-worth. It was no wonder that I went through all the things that I had done in life, because I had no way of knowing that what I went through had affected me the way it did. I also didn't know that my reactions to things weren't "normal" ones either. Like reaching for the bottle when things got bad.

One of the first things the coach asked me was to tell her what I liked doing just for me. I couldn't really answer as I didn't know. I didn't do things for me. I just went along with what others wanted to do. She helped me rediscover myself and realise there were things I could do just for me and that it wasn't selfish to put myself first. We also went over some key moments in my life, and she helped me to reframe my thinking around them. One example was when I didn't get a promotion that I wanted, and it made me feel like a failure. Something I hung onto for a long time. She helped me understand that things happen for a reason, and I wouldn't be on the path I'm on now had I got that promotion. It was all finally making sense. I started implementing things immediately and the transformation in me happened very quickly. It was almost magical to be honest.

It was empowering to say 'no' to people if I no longer wanted to do something, and I felt no guilt in saying it. I started prioritising me time. I made sure I took time out to do things like read a book, have a bubble bath in peace, go and get my nails done or whatever else I felt I needed to do at that time. And what a difference it made. A lot of the changes I made were so simple, but when you aren't aware of what to do in the first place, of course it seems hard. Some things were harder than others, but just like with anything, practice makes perfect. Challenging those negative thoughts was one of them. My immediate reaction for a long time was speaking negatively to myself. So, this meant I had to do a lot of inner work. Every time I noticed a negative thought come up; I would challenge where it had come from. Was it my own thought or had someone said it to me in the past? If someone had said it to me, was it true? By digging deeper each time something came up, I was able to change my thought process and begin thinking in a more positive way.

Once I was feeling in a much better place, I realised that I wanted to give back and help other women to love themselves before they reached crisis point like I did. I studied for my coaching diploma whilst pregnant and then as well as my son, Mind Over Mama was also born. I chose the name because not only is it a clever play on mind over matter, but it is also a reminder that you are more than just a mum. Your mind matters. Your needs matter. YOU matter!! We tend to always put everyone else before us, but at what cost? I tell the women I work with that it isn't selfish to put yourself first. It is a necessity. For example, I know that if I don't take time out for myself to go for a run or do yoga, it affects my mood. And if my mood is affected, then everyone else around me could end up being affected too. So, by doing what I need to do to fill my cup, everyone around me reaps the benefits. It's like a ripple effect.

I use a blend of coaching and Rose Reiki to help empower the women I work with and the transformation in just a few short weeks always makes me so happy. Knowing that these women will not reach the same low point I did, is exactly why I do what I do. And in some ways, it makes what I went through seem worth it. Sounds silly I know, but I often have people say to me that they are sorry for what I went through, but honestly, if I didn't I wouldn't be doing what I am today. I've been guided on this path, and I am thankful I get to speak out and help others along the way.

One thing I will add about self-love is that it is a continuous journey. Just because I feel in a much better place now, doesn't mean I stop working on it. I do things daily that fill up my cup, and I check in with myself regularly. If I am feeling off, I see what needs to be worked on. That's a very important part of the journey too.

There has been another amazing change for me on this journey and that is that I am now sober. The day I found out I was pregnant I stopped drinking without even thinking about it. But once I had my son I started again. Not to the extremes as before, but I could feel it creeping in again on nights out or when my son was with his dad for the weekend.

So, I made the decision to go completely sober as I knew it wasn't doing me any good. I thought, as I had gone 9 months without it before, it would be easy, but it took me 4 or 5 solid attempts to completely stop. There always seemed to be an excuse to drink. A party, a bad day, a good day, anything really. But once I fully committed, really honed in on my reason why, told everyone around me and created my sober Instagram page, it just all clicked into place. I have honestly never been happier. One of the common misconceptions about sobriety is that you will become boring, well I can tell you I am anything but boring. I have danced on tables on a night out, gone to comedy clubs, and I will be going soon to a festival. When you love yourself fully, you soon realise you don't need alcohol to have fun. You are enough as you are!

If I can leave you with some advice, it would be to love yourself the way you deserve to be loved. Put yourself first without feeling guilty, as a happier you will benefit everyone around you. And finally, if you are struggling, reach out and speak to someone. Be it a coach, a friend, the doctor, anyone. Just don't suffer alone. You will get better, and things will be ok. It just might take time!

***

I'm Colette Malcolm, contributing author of the chapter titled 'Self Love isn't Selfish, it's a Necessity'. As a single mother who faced her own mental health challenges, I found a deep-seated desire to uplift and guide others. Today, I stand as a committed advocate for mental health awareness. Having trained as a holistic mindset coach and a Rose Reiki therapist, my mission is to empower fellow mums to realise they encompass more than just the title 'mum'. I'm a huge believer in the transformative power of self-love. My goal is to touch even just one life, hoping that person carries the message forward, creating a ripple effect of positivity. I invite you to discover my story, with the hope that it serves as a testament that nothing is beyond reach.

Follow me @mindovermama

21

CHANGE YOUR STORY
CHANGE YOUR LIFE

Tracey Payne

My heart is thumping hard and fast. My palms are sweaty, and my throat feels so dry. Six thousand pairs of eyes are looking up at me, waiting for me to start talking, and I'm not sure that any sound will come out of my mouth.

I run a successful Network Marketing Business. I lead a fantastic team of incredible men and women. I have travelled the world for free on the most memorable incentive holidays. I have raised my children around the Network Marketing industry and been able to be a full-time present Mum whilst building my business. I have spoken at many events, in audiences large and small. I am living the life I dreamed about and worked hard for. I am confident. I am happy. I am me.

And right now, I am terrified.

When you become what others perceive as 'successful' you can also fall into the 'it's alright for them' bracket. And I had heard the whispers. It's alright for her, she has the confidence to stand at the front of the room. It's alright for her, she finds it easy to talk to people. It's alright for her, she has lots of people around her to support and help. It's alright for her.

It was time to share my story.

I wanted the quiet nervous woman sitting right at the back of the arena to know that she could become the vision she held deep in her heart. That she could overcome any obstacle, get through any challenge, learn, grow, and develop enough to smash through any limiting belief. That she could learn to be confident. That she could learn to be strong. That she could learn to be fearless. I wanted her to know that by changing her story, she could change her life.

Just like I did. But first I had to share where that story started.

The deafening sound of the ambulance sirens, that's what I remember most from that day. The day everything changed. My stepfather was an alcoholic and after another endless fight my mum had taken refuge for the night and gone to keep warm in the garden shed. That's where my older brother found her the next morning, huddled up in a blanket, and where she had suffered a burst aneurysm and passed away in her sleep. Leaving four children aged 2, 5, 7 and 10 in the hands of an abusive alcoholic monster.

Life became a living hell, but over the following years it also became a normal hell.

It was normal to be beaten. It was normal to be used for my stepfather's pleasure, being abused in every way you dare not to imagine. It was normal to be hungry. It was normal to be force fed foods we hated to make us sick. It was normal to creep downstairs at night to steal a spoonful of jam, or a small cup of cornflakes because we hadn't been given any dinner for two days. And when we got caught, it was normal to be whipped with a leather belt and buckle until we bled. It was normal to be scared. It was normal to live in fear.

We still went to school. We still visited other family members. We still had days out. And it's why the horrific abuse went undetected and remained a dirty hidden secret for so long.

Until the day it wasn't a secret anymore.

Have you ever had that feeling in your gut where you can sense that something significant is going to happen? That's how I felt this Thursday, sitting in my science lesson at school. When the classroom door opened and the welfare officer walked in, I just knew he was coming for me. As we walked across the street from the High School to the Junior School where my younger brother and sister were, to discuss an 'incident' that had happened, I just knew everything was about to change.

I was taken into the Head Teachers office, which was full of 9 or 10 other adults looking back at me. My sister had told a friend about our 'normal' home life, and that friend had thankfully told a teacher. And now I was being asked if my stepfather had done the same things to me.

I wanted to say no. I was terrified of being taken away. We had been brainwashed into believing that telling our secret would mean being taken away, and the fear of that unknown reality was far worse than the actual hell we were living.

But I didn't say no. I burst into tears and said yes.

That's the day we became 'carrier bag' children. After my stepfather had been arrested and removed from our house, we were taken home and given 30 minutes to pack what we could into carrier bags. We were all separated and sent off to different forms of care. From that day onwards we have never lived together as siblings again.

I remember my paper round money coming through the letterbox that day £4.23. I gave it to my older brother so that he could get himself some dinner. It would be the last time I saw him for many years.

Life in care was turbulent, and a whole other story to share another time. I spent a long time in children's homes, a mixture of dreadful and then not so dreadful foster homes. Eventually aged 17 I was placed in a bed and breakfast. I had a weekly allowance and two meals a day. I had to put 20p in the shower to get hot water, and 50p in the little electric heater in my bedroom. When I think of my own children now, all having passed the age of 17, I couldn't imagine any of them living that sad existence. It breaks my heart every time I go back to that time in my life. It was the saddest, loneliest, and toughest time.

I remember the empty feeling of having no one to turn to. The sadness that no one cared what I wanted to be in the world.

I hid my fear behind bravado. I pretended I was so much tougher than I really was. My favourite T-shirt said 'this bitch bites' in big black letters across my chest. When in reality inside I was really screaming for somebody to love me and to care for me.

This bravado followed me everywhere. It led to many poor relationship choices, where my sense of poor worth and low self-esteem put me into difficult situations time and time again. This face I put to the world pretending I was strong, fearless, and independent. When I was really a scared little girl.

Having no place to call home led me into the hotel and catering industry as I could work and get board and lodgings. It was here I met my first mentor Mrs Smith. She was the

General Manager of this gorgeous four-star hotel in the Peak District. To many she was an iron lady and feared by the staff who got caught misbehaving. Mrs Smith was the first person who showed me that I had potential. She had high expectations of me, and I wanted to meet them. She put me forward to do my Hotel and Management Degree on a part-time basis at the local University, funded it for me and gave me the extra time off to complete it. For the first time I had something positive to aim for, a goal I could work towards and something to achieve at the end of it. The power of mentorship and my love for helping others was born here. Being the wind beneath someone's wings. Giving them your belief in them until they can build their own. Championing their success and lighting a path for them to follow. Mrs Smith started that passion for me, and although she is no longer with us, I really hope she looks down with pride. Although my career ended up in another direction, it was Mrs Smith who lit that first spark.

I completed that Degree with Distinction. One of four out of 33 people who started and finished the two-year course. The story I told myself was starting to change. I started to believe that it was possible to become something. That I could take charge of my life and the direction it was headed. That I could become my own cheerleader and champion my own success.

But first I had to learn to take charge of my thoughts and my words.

That lesson came a few years later when I was introduced to the Network Marketing industry.

Stumbling into Network Marketing happened when my children were small. My son was four and a half and about to start school and my daughter was six months old. My daughter was born with Turner's Syndrome which led us down a path of hospital appointments, treatments, therapies, and endless worries. I wanted to work, I needed to work but I also wanted to be the one to take care of my children. I still struggled with trusting others, something I would get much better at later in my personal development journey. Network Marketing gave me the option to work from home, with flexible hours, and to step into the world of the Entrepreneur. It gave me the lifeline to be the kind of hands-on Mum I wanted to be, and to facilitate my desire to be a successful businesswoman. I strived to be independent, to rely on no-one but myself. Something that can be a blessing and a curse still to this day.

What I didn't know back then, 17 years ago, was the powerful journey I was going to go on once I was introduced to Personal Development. I have always loved reading, as a child it was a form of escape. I wanted to disappear into the land of Narnia through my wardrobe and to live in the Faraway Tree deep in the enchanted forest. So being told to read by my business mentor excited me. Until she told me to read a book called 'Attitude is Everything' By Jeff Keller.

I always thought I had the 'Right Attitude' until this book showed me that I had 'a *right* attitude'. For the first time I started to understand how my past was impacting my future. I might have been able to step away from the abuse on the outside, but on the inside, I was telling myself so many disempowering stories, that I was sabotaging my own chance of success. I was looking at life through dirty windows that were marked with the mud of my past. I had to learn to talk to myself again, and to clean those windows bit by bit, and to stop throwing more mud on them. I had to learn a new language that was going to empower me.

I was introduced to incredible Mentors through books and on-line learnings. Some of the most impactful being speakers such as Tony Robbins, Jim Rohn, Zig Ziglar, Les Brown, John Maxwell, and countless others. I turned my car into a mobile library, absorbing hours of content on CD's driving up and down the country building my business and attending appointments. Their words became my words. And as I tell my team daily, what goes in must come out. Garbage In, garbage out. Good words in, good words out.

What followed was a love of learning. Still to this day I get a new book pop through my letterbox every month. It's even easier now with podcasts, YouTube, social media, and free resources.

As I started to learn new words my thoughts changed and became more positive. As my thoughts changed my actions got bigger and better. Once my actions got bigger my results got better. And as my results grew so did my business, so did my confidence and ultimately so did my life.

Surrounding yourself with the right people is so important and something that has been key to my success and is fundamental in my ongoing success. We can not always choose our family and there are always going to be people in your life who are not the best influence on you, but always remember that you get to choose how much time you give them. Protect your mind at all costs, don't just let anyone go walking through there.

It wasn't easy. It still isn't easy. There are times when I still doubt myself. Imposter Syndrome rears its ugly head more times than I want it too, especially with social media. But I have learned to surround myself with people who remind me of who I am. I recognise the signs when this is happening, and I remind myself not to compare my day 1 to their day 500. I also remind myself that the life and challenges I face today would have been my dream life six months ago. Stay on the journey, it is not the end destination, but the journey that fills our heart.

So, as I stand on stage my heart beating fast, about to share this story with 6000 of my peers, I look out across the audience and know I have a powerful message to share. A message of hope, of strength and of courage.

I want them to know the little girl I was.

I want them to know her journey.

I want them to understand that a terrible past does not mean a terrible future.

I want them to feel her pain and to experience her breakthroughs.

I want them to know she worked so hard for the success and the confidence that they see so easily today.

I want them to know that anything is possible if you want it enough and work hard for it.

I want them to know that they can too.

Your past does not define your future. Change Your Story to Change Your Life

***

So happy to meet you, I'm Tracey, a Mum, a Network Marketing Professional and all-round gin loving, cocktail drinking pretty decent person (after a coffee). Being a part of this collaboration means so much. Bringing all these amazing women together to help you find your voice too. I am so thrilled to share my story with you. I hope it empowers you to push through your own limiting beliefs, and to see the strength and power you have inside you. You are capable of so much; your past does not define your future. In my chapter I share with you how you can change

your story, to change your life.
You can find me here linktr.ee/TraceyPayne

You Are Stronger Than You Give Yourself Credit For

Louise Fletcher

Sometimes in life, we find the courage to make monumental changes. We feel fear but we do it anyway. We think it will be the answer to all our prayers and in some ways it is. But in truth, we still have so much work to do but everything that happens makes us stronger. The decision you make is simply the beginning. The point when we say 'Enough is enough' is the first step on the road to rediscovery. And once we take that step, we have so much growth ahead of us. Take my story for instance.

In early 2019 I found myself in a place where I was in this constant daily battle. Married to a great guy but knowing we were on completely different pages was breaking me daily. But my issue was, I didn't have the confidence to open my mouth and be completely truthful. The year before I had broached the subject that I was not happy but from fear of the unknown and not wanting to hurt those directly around us, I swept my feelings under the carpet.

In early 2019, bigger cracks appeared and my resentment towards my husband took me to the breaking point. This completely broke me. He was my safe place, my rock. But as I observed things, I saw he was so fulfilled in his life, and I was not. He loved his job; he always worked extra hours and went over and beyond to be a great role model. Work was also his social life and even though there were cracks in our marriage I could see how fulfilled he was by what we had built in the way of material possessions. It was the complete opposite for me.

All I had ever wanted was to be a Mum. I was lucky enough to have a beautiful baby boy in 1992 from a previous relationship – my shining star, but sadly he passed away after 6 days. You see I had come from a broken family and all I ever wanted was to create my own family and have safety. I had even played the role of step-mum twice and absolutely loved it, but in both those relationships I had my heart broken when my partners at the time decided more children had been taken off the table for them, this was after a few years of living together. So, when I met my ex-husband, and he asked me to marry him I made it clear I wanted to be a Mum. Fast forward and in 10 years of marriage we had created safety but unfortunately, the children part did not happen. I won't go into the details of all the avenues I explored, which were met with a no, as that is not why I am sharing this story. Life can sometimes have different plans for us, and this is what I want to share more about. I want to share how having an unknown amount of courage and taking a huge leap of faith can open a whole new world of happiness. So, for me leaving my marriage was THE most difficult decision of my whole life. The last thing I wanted to do was cause heartache to others, but in staying I would have been causing myself more heartache. In March/April of 2019, I had a breakdown – I was so completely lost. I had to express my feelings.

It was painful to say I thought it was the end of the marriage. But when I look back now, I was setting us both free. My husband was at the end of his tether at the downward spiral I constantly found myself on. But what happened from my courage far surpassed my wildest dreams. I went to Boa Vista Cape Verde at the end of October 2019 as this had become my place of peace over the years and families had surrounded us with so much love. I went to stay with my darling Karina and her son Rendy to take time out but also with a dream in my heart to help impact the lives of the children in Boa Vista. The next part is still a pinch-me moment.

On the 3rd of January 2020, I heard about a friend of Karina's who was opening a much-needed kindergarten in the village of Rabil, which was the village Karina had lived in all her life. The moment I heard the full story and the vision I knew I could help. This date was also a special date when I looked back as it was the 3rd of January 2013 that I had first stepped foot in Boa Vista – even in that moment I knew this island was special. The kindergarten had achieved so much but they needed some help with the final equipment so they could open their doors.

Initially, I was asked if I would sponsor a child, but I knew I could do so much more! I opened a Facebook group and reached out to everyone I knew, and donations started to come in, plus via a friend who worked for TUI there were donation boxes placed in Manchester and Birmingham crew rooms and in addition to the toys left in the boxes some of the air hostesses kindly brought from their own homes, clothes and toys their children no longer used. At the same time as I heard about the kindergarten project, I received a phone call from a friend to say they knew of someone selling an apartment in Boa Vista and asked if I would be interested. The apartment was a little one-bed apartment with an ocean view. It was like these 2 things had been hand-delivered to me.

For the next 2 months, all the stops were pulled out and the kindergarten's inauguration party was 29th February 2020. It was all systems go until the news that covid 19 had been brought to the island. Within days the hotels were closed, and all the repatriation flights took all the holidaymaker's home. I thought this would be for a few weeks, but the hotels remained closed until October 2021. For 19 months I then helped to raise funds for food donations and on average we helped around 80 to 100 families per month.

In the last 6 months of this time, I really started to struggle, not only with my energy levels but also, I felt the pressure to keep everything going, as once I had started to help, I wasn't able to stop. I felt the families needed help and I was able to raise the funds, so I had to keep going. I could have easily stopped as I was in a fortunate position as I had my divorce settlement to live on. I could have sat back and just had the much-needed time out to recover from the breakdown of my marriage, but something kept me going and each month money would be donated.

In October 2021 the hotels slowly started to open again, and some normality was resumed. I was able to stop the food donation as by this time I was really tired, but I carried on supporting the kindergarten finding sponsors, and at that time, teaching English. What I didn't realise at the time was that my kidney function had started to decline. I had also had an episode of chest pains but after paying for tests nothing showed up. The doctor put it down to diet. So as the island opened up and things started to get back to normal, I was apprehensive. This quiet island I had lived on and enjoyed throughout the pandemic was about to change. This was where my next challenges were ready to greet me. And this is why I said at the beginning, the first decision you make is just the beginning.

For me, this was a time that so much was brought to the surface that I hadn't dealt with. I had buried my head in the kindergarten project and the pandemic and was so busy serving others. This was where the really tough inner work started. I believe that as we level up in our healing journey, we are brought new challenges and boy oh boy was I brought new challenges.

Around the beginning of 2022 changes were happening and whilst I was still accommodating certain situations, I found myself being triggered and stuff from my earlier years coming to the surface. I started to go downhill and in May 2022 I had another mini breakdown. Everything hit me like a tonne of bricks. I took myself off to one of the little villages to take some much-needed time out and to find my thoughts. I felt like things were crashing around me. My place of peace was being challenged. And in addition to all of that, I was working through the stuff that had reared its ugly head again. For the rest of 2022, I really had to work on my self-care. It was an uphill battle.

In the summer of 2022, just after the kindergarten graduation party, I returned to the UK to stay with friends and enjoy some holidays and attend my hospital visits at the renal clinic. This was good for my soul. And during this time, I created a journal that I sell on Amazon called Rise and Shine. This journal is all about the S.H.I.N.E.S. principles that were born whilst out in Boa Vista. My business is called Shine With Lou so the acronym fits well. These were my 6 daily morning disciplines to start my day off right.

S.H.I.N.E.S. is an acronym for:

- See It – Your vision.
- Handwritten – Journaling.
- Inner Connections – Prayer, meditation, or silence.
- New Ideas – Podcast, audiobooks, or something that feeds your mind with positivity.
- Elevate Energy – Exercise or simply dance around the kitchen.
- Say It – Affirmations.

Spending just one minute on each discipline each morning will help to move you in a more positive direction and these were the disciplines that, when done, make a difference.

During my time in the UK, I learned that my kidney function had dropped by 9%. This was a complete shock, but as I have had this condition for over 30 years, I brushed it off. They advised it was time for me to be on the kidney transplant list. I was still in denial – in fact, I still am. I went back to Boa Vista in December, still struggling with my energy levels and not quite feeling right but then went into Christmas mode. I had saved some money to donate to the Christmas party at the kindergarten but as a sponsor had dropped out a few months before, the decision was made for the funds to be used to complete the sponsorship for a little girl for the remaining year. So, in my usual fashion, I got on Facebook, explained the situation and within a short amount of time we had enough money to hold a big party not just for the kindergarten in Rabil but for all the children in the village. This was a fabulous party. Zeny, the owner of O'Encanto baked around 7 cakes to cater to all the children and a team of ladies from the village made 150+ burgers all from a tiny room – they were amazing! We even had enough funds left over for Zeny and her team to hold a party in another village for the elders a few days later.

The children's party was spectacular, but I really struggled. My kidney health was declining, and my body was telling me I couldn't take part as I had before. For the next few days, I was wiped out. Around this time, I came across a modality called Belief Coding and I was intrigued. I heard it was a healing modality and I was willing to try anything to help my kidneys and deal with what had reared its head in 2022. I returned to the UK at the end of January 2023 to attend a 3-day event and begin immersing myself in this new modality. Then at the beginning of February, I went for a routine heart check so that I could be placed on the kidney transplant list only to find out I had angina. I had been struggling the last few years since I had the tests at the hospital, but I just thought it was the humidity. And again, this is why I say our decisions are just the start. We still have curveballs that life throws at us. But I firmly believe that if we practise self-care and slow our lives down, we can deal with whatever life throws at us. We are stronger than we realise and I have proven that to myself.

This is why I say our initial decisions are just the start. I am embracing what life has for me and I know whatever happens I will get through this. I have in the past and I will do it again, and so will you! I am excited and optimistic about what my future holds as I know I have the tools to deal with any curveballs head on! I firmly believe that if we practise self-care, slow our lives down and remove the drama we can deal with whatever life throws at us. We are stronger than we realise, and I have proven that to myself. I may be in the UK now because of health issues and this has caused me no end of distress because I have rebuilt my life in Boa Vista but what I do have is so much joy in my heart from loved ones in Boa Vista and of course from the children at the kindergarten. If I'd never taken that leap of faith, I would not have been blessed with so much love, and knowing I helped to make a difference in the lives of the children in O'Encanto over the last 3 years. If things are a challenge for you at the moment, have a look at what you can introduce into your daily routine to help you keep your head above water just like I did.

Much love & light

Lou xox

***

Introducing Louise Fletcher, a captivating individual whose life radiates with positivity and an unyielding enthusiasm, despite encountering a series of unexpected challenges. With an unwavering spirit, Louise has become a beacon of inspiration for others, consistently demonstrating resilience and a zest for life that remains unshaken. Louise's journey is intricately woven with the threads of her personalised S.H.I.N.E.S. Principles and her passion for Belief Coding® which weaves through her triumphant journey, a testament to transformative principles. Louise's narrative lights life's path.

www.iamlouisefletcher.co.uk

AN EMPOWERED EMPATH

Lisa Williams

You are not too sensitive, beautiful one. You are an empath, a word I wish I knew and understood when I was a child and a young adult. I often wonder how much unnecessary pain I could have avoided. It took me nearly 37 years around the sun to embrace all of the magic that comes with being an empath and what has led me here to this moment in time.

I now realise that I was meant to go through all the pain in my past so I can now fully stand in my power and empower other beautiful, sensitive empath souls to understand that there is true empowerment in being an empath. Giving you tips and tools to guide you on this journey. Guiding you on how you can protect your energy and still be a beacon of love and light for others.

LET'S BEGIN WITH MY JOURNEY

As a child, I was always told that I was too sensitive, too kind, too soft.

I would pick up on the energies around me.

I would actually feel the physical pain of others and I didn't at the time understand that it wasn't my own pain or energy.

I could feel the sadness radiating from a TV screen picking up on any news.

I would go to bed every night and be wondering how I could make the world a better place.

I felt like it was my job to do so, I spent most of my life this way.

Feeling like it was up to me. to create a better world.

And in some respects it is......Although now I've realised, I can make a difference in making this world a better place, but I don't need to carry the weight of it on my shoulders.

Can you relate?

Understanding who we truly are on a soul level, giving ourselves that love and kindness and the most beautiful word of all, acceptance and my beautiful one together we will flourish.

The journey to finding oneself can seem never-ending but the most important thing you can do is have love in your heart and embrace who you truly are in each and every phase of your life. Whatever you've been through up until this point in your life, and whatever phase you are in right now in your life, or wherever you are on your healing journey.

Let's take a moment to acknowledge that by placing your hand on your heart taking a deep breath in and exhale and let it go.

Get Comfortable And Let's Dive Right In

As I said I spent nearly 37 years around the sun not understanding I wasn't broken. I am an empath. For so long, the world's emotions weighed on me like a relentless storm, drowning me in waves of anxiety, joy, sorrow, and anger that wasn't even mine. I was a ship lost at sea, adrift in a tempest of feelings, unable to find my own identity amidst the emotional turbulence of others.

It all started when I was a child, a sensitive soul who could sense the slightest shifts in mood around me. At first, I thought everyone could do this, but as I grew older, I realised I was different. My family and those around me couldn't comprehend the depth of my empathy, dismissing it as an overactive imagination or mere sympathy. They couldn't feel the currents of emotion running through me like electric charges, connecting me to the very essence of those around me. In school, I was labelled as overly emotional and weird. The other kids teased me, and even some teachers misunderstood my sensitivity, believing I lacked resilience.

I became used to hiding my true self, wearing a mask of indifference to protect myself from the overwhelming emotional onslaught that accompanied me every day.

As the years passed, I grew accustomed to this self-imposed isolation. I was a master of reading people, picking up on their unspoken words and hidden feelings. I had an uncanny ability to understand their pain and bring comfort, yet I could never share my own burden. It was a lonely existence, and I yearned to find someone who could see beyond the façade I presented to the world.

After living this way of not truly understanding why I always felt such strong energy around me, and over three decades of being a compulsive people pleaser, BOOM! October 2017 hit me with the weight of the world, never feeling like I fitted in anywhere. Even after nearly 20 years of running a successful dance and theatre school, and having a wonderful husband and daughter I wanted out, out from this world, this pain. And on the 17th of October 2017, I started to write my goodbye note, feeling that the world would be better off without me.

My husband found me crying and shaking in the corner of our bedroom holding the note in my hand. As he read the note I remember the look of sadness in his eyes showing the question of how he could have not known that I felt this way. He held me tightly and we both cried. He begged that I seek out help and apologised for not seeing the signs.

I agreed to get help, so I called my GP. As I arrived with my heart feeling like it was wanting to burst through my chest, I entered the room and felt my whole life flash before me as I said the words "I don't want to live anymore." Just saying that out loud to a stranger actually felt like a weight had been lifted.

I was offered Antidepressants, but something inside of me felt that wasn't the right path for me.

As I walked back home on a cold, overcast day, with many tears in my eyes suddenly the sun pierced through the clouds, and a powerful message was guided to me.

There was still light, love, hope, and purpose within me.

THE ROSE QUARTZ AND REBIRTH.

Just a few days or so later my daughter who was nine at the time wanted to visit the local museum and as children often do she wanted to visit the gift shop. That shop was so magical to her, so bright, so beautiful, she spotted a display of crystals and she was in complete awe of them like they were radiating some sort of magic. She chose to buy some. And from out of nowhere I heard a voice whisper telling me to pick up a Rose Quartz.

That evening I researched crystals. I started to look into their meanings and their healing properties. I slept with a rose quartz every evening under my pillow or on my heart. I had such a deep loving connection that I had not felt before. It's like I started to love and accept myself again. I started to heal. That rose quartz became more than a crystal.

I started to practise daily gratitude, meditation, affirmations, and self-love. I completely immersed myself in learning this new spiritual and holistic way of healing and the more I healed the more my desire was to help others heal too. The universe started to show me many beautiful signs and synchronicities of seeing Angel numbers like 1111, it was literally everywhere, then robins, white feathers, butterflies and so much more.

As I continued to open myself up to the guidance, I decided to study to become a life coach and mindfulness practitioner which that, and 38 years of life experience have led me on this beautiful spiritual path and most divine guidance shows up for me now through whispers to number sequences, guides and through mentors.

And then as they say "When the student is ready the teacher will appear".

In the forms of mentors, books, and women both in the physical form and spirit came to me.

It was February 2019 when I heard a whisper that I would be able to heal people with my hands and with spoken words and intention and just like all the divine guidance, my Reiki Master came into my life.

During my third attunement, I had an out-of-body experience. It was the most blissful, wonderful experience. I was with my Nan who has now passed on. I couldn't hear everything she said except to believe in myself that I am here to do great things.

When my Reiki Master touched my feet and brought me

back into my body I cried. It was the most incredible feeling. At that moment more than any other moment in my life it confirmed my mission to help other women unlock their magic and unleash their power.

And from that day my beautiful Nanny Peggy has been my spirit guide. She has since given me so much guidance.

"There's no need to hide," she said, her voice like a gentle breeze. "You're an empath, a beautiful, rare gift in this world. Embrace it."

I am so blessed to have her as my spirit guide as she shows up for me in all the moments that I need her and has even shown up to help others too. She was a beautiful blessing in my life and in this way now continues to live on.

With lots of inner work and my beautiful Nanny Peggy's guidance, I have learned to shield myself from the overwhelming emotional baggage that had haunted me for so long. I found strength in being able to understand between my emotions and those of others. No longer lost in the turbulent sea of feelings. I started to find my tribe of people who accepted me for who I was and celebrated my empathic nature. I finally shed the mask I had worn for so long and embraced who I was at the core. I was no longer in fear of my own emotions or those of the world.

As I ventured deeper into the world of inner healing, shadow work, learning, and unlearning, I knew I wanted to create a community where women who are spiritual, empaths, healers, and lightworkers could be together holding space for each other and being celebrated for who we truly are, removing the masks, burning the boxes of what society says we should be. And So Spiritual Sisters Collective was birthed into the world in October 2022.

I learned that I could use my gift to create profound

connections with others, heal their wounds, and foster understanding and compassion. But I also understood the importance of taking care of myself, of retreating into solitude when necessary, to recharge and rejuvenate my own spirit.

Now, as I stand in my 40th year around the Sun it's a new chapter in my life, I no longer see myself as broken. I am an empath, and I have a purpose—to bring light to the darkest corners of the human experience and to remind others that they are not alone. I am a vessel of empathy, and through the currents of emotion that flow within me, I will make a difference in this world, one heart at a time.

As an empath, it's essential to protect your energy and maintain emotional well-being, especially in environments that can be overwhelming or draining.

HERE ARE FIVE TOP TIPS TO HELP YOU PROTECT YOUR ENERGY:

- Set Boundaries: Establish clear boundaries with others to prevent emotional overload. Learn to say "no" when necessary and prioritise your needs. Recognise that it's okay to take time for yourself and not absorb the emotions or problems of everyone around you.
- Practice Self-Care: Engage in self-care activities that nourish your mind, body, and soul. This may include meditation, dance, yoga, music, spending time in nature, reading, journaling, or any other activities that help you feel grounded and rejuvenated.
- Identify Energy Drains: Be super mindful of people, places, or situations that drain your energy. Limit your exposure to them whenever possible and surround yourself with positive and uplifting individuals who understand and respect your empathic nature.

- Visualise Protection: Use visualisation techniques to create a protective shield around yourself. Imagine a bubble of white or golden light surrounding you, serving as a barrier that allows positive energy to flow in but blocks out negative or overwhelming emotions.
- Practise Emotional Detachment: While empathy is a beautiful trait, it's so important to learn how to detach emotionally when needed. Remind yourself that you cannot solve everyone›s problems or take on their emotions. Practice observing and supporting others without absorbing their energy.

Please remember, it's an ongoing process but one that I believe is so important for our well-being.

The world needs you.

The Light within me can see and celebrates the Light within you.

Lisa x

***

Lisa Williams is a multi-passionate entrepreneur who is dedicated to guiding and uplifting others on their spiritual journeys, as a Spiritual Empowerment Mentor, Founder of Spiritual Sisters Collective, Dance teacher and amp; podcast host at Raw and amp; Real with Lisa Williams. Lisa has over 25 years of experience in business and leadership. Beyond her spiritual pursuits, Lisa's love for dance is equally important. She believes in the power of movement as a means of expression, healing, and personal growth. Through dance she encourages others to tap into their creativity and embody their emotions freely. Lisa's journey has been guided by her own experiences, challenges, and self-discovery. She wholeheartedly believes that everyone has the potential to transform their lives and discover their inner light. Her story is her inspiration for her continued work and dedication. 'I am over the moon to share some of my story with you in this book'. 'The light within me can see and celebrates the light within you'.

You can be in Lisa's world and follow her journey by connecting with her at:

https://spiritualsisterscollective.vipmembervault.com

and Raw & amp; Real with Lisa Williams:

https://rawrealwithlisawilliams.buzzspout.com/

FINDING MY VOICE

Janine McDonald

I'd gone to a friend's house to play in her den which was the outhouse in her back yard. In huge letters on the wall it said 'Janine is ......' I was around 9 years old. I pretended I'd not seen it. I honestly don't know how because the letters were massive! My friends didn't acknowledge it either. I can't remember what that last word actually was, but I do know it was derogatory, unfair, and uncalled for. I started berating myself for not dealing with the situation at the time, for not using my voice. I remained silent pretending it hadn't happened.

High school was a difficult time for me too. Often left out of social activities, and parties. Feeling like I was always in my older sister's shadow, not having my own identity. Teachers referred to me as Alison's Sister. I wanted to shout NO! I'm Janine! I'm Me! Instead, I quietly accepted it. My voice was buried deep down inside me.

I allowed two managers at work to bully me. They were undertaking a job-share role and both worked in completely different ways. The same applications were to be submitted to them in divergent formats with different attachments. Often, I would be accused of not doing what they'd asked me to do, when in fact I had. When I did raise the courage to speak up to a senior manager about their behaviour along with discussing my exams, I was met the next morning with one of those managers taking me straight into a room and threatening me, banging papers repeatedly on the desk and demanding to know why I had spoken. I didn't use my voice. I cowered on the chair and allowed the verbal abuse to continue and swallow me up.

Working on secondment to a branch in Northern Ireland, I was praised for being knowledgeable and thanked for supporting the team to their successes. I was promoted to manager of the flagship branch and took on additional responsibilities. During the Awards night, I didn't receive an award, but I didn't expect to, it was OK. What really riled me was that I wasn't even acknowledged. Nothing mentioned about the training I'd created and implemented, the improvement in systems, the security aspects which combined significantly contributed to the success of the branch. I was an outsider. No fun, unable to take a joke. Even the auditors said that I was being unfairly treated. Once again, I felt stifled and suffocated by the wrongdoing of others. My voice was quiet.

Just 3 days into my honeymoon, the phrase 'You really are stupid aren't you!' was shouted at me. We were walking along a path from the apartment to the reception area of the hotel and it continued to be a video playing in my mind over and over again. Over the next few years, the constant emotional barrage took its toll. I no longer had a whisper let alone a voice. I became withdrawn and down on myself. I felt responsible for everything and everyone. The cooking, cleaning, education, school runs, shopping, the car servicing, the household repairs, the garden. Going shopping for food would cause me to panic in the middle of the store. I woke up in the night sobbing 'but we don't have any potatoes'.

Work was extremely busy and stressful. A member of my team's husband committed suicide and I was to inform her. It was Valentine's Day. Her Dad had come to the office and I knew immediately it was something serious. This was the second time I'd had to deal with loss of life of a team member's family in this way. It hit me hard. I couldn't forget the role I felt I'd played in further destroying their lives. I spoke to my manager. He just said 'You shouldn't get too close to the team' I retreated further into my shell.

Not knowing how to deal with that first situation at Primary School, not being aware that I had tools within me to rise up and shine has, I believe, affected me my whole life and the feeling of not having a voice. Not being listened to. The feeling that my opinions don't matter.

We now had two very small children, the youngest of which didn't sleep much at night. I was exhausted and depressed. I further lost my identity and slid deeper and deeper inside myself. I no longer recognised the person I was. Completely withdrawn, I was only just surviving. I didn't speak up.

Many memories were flooding back to me. The traumas, the stigma, not standing up for myself. The clutter began building up. I'd sweep things which were on surfaces and sofas into a carrier bag thinking 'I'll sort that when they've gone', which of course I didn't and before I knew it I had about seven huge bags full of things to sort out. The overwhelm was real. I'd once again lost my voice in all this mess. It built up even more to the point where I could hardly get into the spare room.

I remember sitting on the sofa looking at a small pile of toys in the corner of the room, telling myself that it's only going to take 5 minutes to tidy them away. The other part of my brain however, had other ideas. It was rendering me powerless and paralysed, not allowing me to get up and take action.

I'd only just returned to work after my second daughter was born only to be rushed into the hospital with an excruciating gallbladder pain and a cancer scare. The doctors were trying to co-ordinate so that they would only need to operate once. I was still breastfeeding so had the added pressure of using a pump, storing the milk and then someone collecting it within a short timeframe. Thankfully, the cancer was a scare and I only needed my gallbladder removing. After which both my daughters had chickenpox as did I, twice, and then I had a really bad chest infection. All of this was happening whilst I was studying photography at evening college as I had a feeling that redundancies were coming at work.

In 2014 I was made redundant from my only employment of 24 years and 10 months. My redundancy payment went on repaying debts my ex built up along with having to remortgage the house. I was now on benefits. I was lost.

The clutter was building again. Not just toys and clothes but paperwork too. Letters from Child Tax Credits. I remember shaking every time a brown envelope dropped through the letterbox. I couldn't open them. At times we were receiving 3 a day. All the same date but all saying we owed different amounts. Significant amounts. I realised that I had to take control. No-one else would. I spoke to MIND who listened to my issues and made phone calls on my behalf. They helped me set up a payment plan, one which I'll still be paying into my seventies! All this stress due to a simple administrative error on my employer's part.

At home, I started to say to myself 'Just three things' just pick up three things, it doesn't matter what they were. Just any three things in front of me and either pack them away, recycle them or donate them. Over time, and by this, I mean a long time, I cleared the spare room. I moved onto the DOOM bags, I didn't realise that's what they were called until recently and, it's a common neurodivergent trait. I sorted the paperwork in to piles. The envelopes to recycling along with the leaflets, the paperwork which required shredding and that which needed action. I transferred to online bills and bank statements to ease the paperwork and post going forward and made sure we had the correct insurances in place. Slowly I started to see space on the floor! This gave me incentive to continue. I'd reward myself with a hot chocolate or a TV programme. Can you guess what I found at the bottom of the pile of things in the room? A duster. Oh, the irony.

There was the time, I can remember exactly when and where. We were sat in the car on the drive and I was wanting to shout out 'Just Leave!' but my voice remained in my head. Why couldn't I say it out loud? My self-confidence was now at absolute rock bottom and I was struggling to function.

As my confidence grew, my voice grew louder. I was empowering myself to build a greater future for myself and my girls. I'd spent too long suppressing the words which needed to be said. It took me 4 years to say those words which had been in my head. I arranged for our home to be sold and my husband and I split up.

My daughters and I went to live with a friend. Mattresses on the floor in a small room but we were happy. My car became my storage unit. In those 12 months, she nurtured us inside and out with nutritious food, emotional support, and laughter. We helped each other and still do. We both know that if either of us needed anything in the middle of the night, we'd be there for each other. Her amazing and unwavering support has helped me become the person I am today.

I was declared fit for work. I was ready. However, companies thought otherwise. Rejection after rejection. No-one wanted me. They thought that I would want a career quickly after starting when what I actually needed was a job with hours where I could pick the girls up from school and take time off in school holidays as childcare wasn't available, and I was now a single parent. They didn't seem to understand that my life was now totally different.

My mental wellbeing was declining again and clutter started building up around our new home. Everything had returned from storage, but we didn't have anywhere to put it. I was supporting others with sorting out their homes rather than sorting my own and avoiding my own issues. Again, I started my 'Just 3 Things' and I began to understand that when a partnership separates, a grieving process can occur. In the majority of cases, one party sets up a new home having taken hardly any possessions with them, creating a new way of living. This leaves the other partner with not just the material possessions, but the emotional aspects of them too. It's extremely difficult to move forward when you have the baggage of the past on your shoulders seeing it all around you all day every day. Slowly I am moving forward. Replacing items and creating a home with items I love and cherish.

Those memories which had adversely affected me throughout my whole life were now being addressed and I am finding my voice.

I have always felt fulfilled when helping and supporting others. Always have and always will as Acts of Service are part of my love language.

I now use my voice and life experiences to empower and help others. To support families struggling with clutter and disorganisation gain time and freedom in a much calmer home by removing the overwhelm. To give them a Clear Home, Clear Head, Clear Heart. They deserve it. I don't judge because, as you've read, I struggle with clutter myself. I know what it's like to be overwhelmed. To juggle so many different priorities in difficult circumstances. I'm by your side. I listen to your voice and listen to your story.

I founded my business, Clear the Clutter Now in March 2020, 3 weeks before the world went into Lockdown. Never before had we experienced anything like it. I couldn't go into people's home to support them so I used my voice to make changes in other areas. I spoke out about setting up a business from a mental wellbeing perspective and having to alter the way I worked virtually from setting up. I networked with people I'd never met before and made connections all over the UK and overseas. I used my voice to share my own journey with clutter by guest speaking in many different groups and organisations providing inspiration and motivation to many. I also set up online decluttering sessions for support. My voice is now strong and loud.

I've won awards, been finalists in others and featured in over thirty publications worldwide. I'm a champion of others to overcome their silence in their issues so that they can live a fulfilled life. I use the silent voice from my past to create a positive and driven future for myself, my family, and my business.

We all have our own story. A story we WILL change together. We WILL evolve. We WILL use our voices. We WILL be heard.

I use my voice to change people's lives.

***

Janine McDonald feels her voice has been suppressed throughout her life. Struggling with her mental wellbeing later in life and with a messy home she is now ardent about using her life experiences and her voice to support others.

She is passionate about supporting professionals and families struggling with clutter and disorganisation gain time and freedom in a much calmer home by removing the overwhelm. Janine shares her story to lift others up and inspire them to make small changes to make a big difference.

You can find Janine at www.clearthecluternow.co.uk

Shame, Guilt, And Gaslighting, 'You Know It's All Your Fault!'

Michelle Louise Smith

*name changed to provide anonymity

The aim of my story is to bring awareness to domestic violence, that it happens more than people realise, that not everyone has a voice, or feels brave, courageous, bold enough to speak up. Survivors fear what will happen if they do speak up, tell someone, will they be believed? Will they get the support needed to enable them to build a new life? Will they leave the house alive? That is certainly something I wasn't sure of towards the end of the abusive relationship, but I knew that no matter what, I couldn't live a lie anymore for my sake and for the sake of my children. My son witnessed things, my daughter was too young, how could I allow them to witness their mother being beaten, I knew that I wanted to be a positive role model for both of them. I want to inspire at least one person. I want them to know that there is hope and life after abuse.

My story starts in May 2005, I had come out of a long-term relationship, I had been with my husband for 14 years and married for nearly 8. I became a single mum to a little boy aged 2, I was recovering from a major Rheumatoid Arthritis flare, which left me unable to care for myself, and had been triggered by the pregnancy. At this point I was in recovery and back on my feet due to starting medication, so I moved out of the marital home and rented my Dads' house.

I started a new relationship with a man called Ben*, he reeled me in by telling me a sob story about his ex-wife cheating on him when he was in the Army. He told me he was an ex-Paratrooper, had been in conflict and seen horrific things, which he loved to talk about when drunk! Oh and he'd lived this amazing, fabulous lifestyle, travelling the world, visiting luxury hotels and restaurants, well that was until we met! Then he was a penniless delivery driver, who quit his job.

I fell hook, line and sinker, I felt totally smitten by him, he was a charmer and I believed every word that came out of his mouth.

In June 2005, we went away, it was my first holiday to Malta, and our first holiday together. We had both been drinking on the aeroplane, and we were both sozzled. We were on the way to the hotel in the minibus continuing to drink alcohol, when suddenly out of nowhere I got a slap in the face. I was so shocked and surprised I didn't believe it had happened. I asked him about it, and he denied anything had happened, he said I had imagined it I started to wonder if I had. I got upset about it but chose to put it to the back of my mind. We spent 2 weeks drinking a lot, arguing a lot and spending my money. If only I had paid attention.

In March 2006, the settlement from my previous marriage came through and I was able to buy a house for me and my son. In June 2006 I bought my house, a 2 bed town house. My son and I moved in, and I asked Ben* to move into my house too, naively I thought he would be like my ex-husband, trustworthy, honest and hard-working, I couldn't have been any further from the truth!!

At this point in my life, I was still very vulnerable, having been very poorly with my Arthritis flare, then splitting up with my husband who was my first long term relationship. I felt responsible for Ben*. He didn't have a job and had moved down from Yorkshire to Derbyshire. I wanted to rescue him, be the one who looked after him, regardless of how he treated me. I allowed him to be a secondary card holder on my credit cards, he started using them and my debit cards, spending my money on going to the pub, and getting drunk, disappearing, he also obtained cash from the ATM on the credit cards. Not long after he moved in, he got a temporary job at a call centre, he hated it. One particular day he went to work, I never thought anything of it. I got worried when he didn't come home and tried to contact him, but his phone was switched off, he never came home that evening. I didn't sleep very well, I had the Police turn up on my doorstep asking me if I had given Ben* permission to drive my car, I said 'yes', he was caught drunk in charge of a vehicle!! He hadn't been to work at all, he had been drinking all day and ended up getting caught behind the wheel, I never found out the truth as he wouldn't tell me!!

I thought marriage would be a salvation for Ben*. He asked me around July 2006, and I said 'yes'. We went to Las

Vegas to do it in September 2006. I paid for everything, and even on our wedding night he was chatting up the waitresses, I couldn't handle it, so I walked off. He let me go off. I had to go and find him in the end, I was drunk, upset, and knew this was a huge mistake, yet I still loved him. He ignored me for the rest of our stay. He sat drinking and wouldn't engage with me, I felt so alone, I had no idea what to do. I stuck it out of course, and when we got home, I caught him cheating. I found him in a pub drinking wine with a young girl on one occasion and I still took him back!

In February 2008 I found out I was pregnant, I had come off all of my Rheumatoid Arthritis medication to get pregnant as I thought a child would be the next best thing to bring Ben* around to being a decent man! He loved my son and was good with him, so I naively thought he would love his own child! Even though I was pregnant he still hit me, gave me 2 black eyes and punched me after I found out I was pregnant! I stopped drinking, but I comfort ate instead and for 2, as I became bigger it antagonised Ben* and he was really nasty to me, calling me names even more. In October 2008 my daughter was born by C section, she was gorgeous. Ben* absolutely doted on her and I thought this was it! He managed about 3 weeks of being loving towards me before the abuse started again, only this time it was worse as I had put a lot of weight on!

Between 2008-2010 I struggled with my weight. It was constantly up and down! I was drinking heavily again and not eating, this was my coping strategy with the abuse I was suffering. I didn't tell anyone, I made out my life was perfect and amazing, even my best friends had no idea or so I thought!! On several occasions I had phoned one best friend saying that I had been pinned to the door by my throat, and

Ben* had tried to strangle me, yet I also said it was ok as he let me go! He would call me mental, say I was psychotic and hysterical, he would call me moody and get my son to join in. He would use that as an excuse to go out drinking. He would deliberately turn his phone off so I couldn't get hold of him, or he wouldn't come home from work. He would check my phone, and read messages off friends, he even threatened to contact social services and have the children taken off me because I was so psychotic and mental.

The straw that broke the camel's back came early September 2010. I finally snapped and had enough when he smashed a picture frame over my head, my daughter in my arms, she was screaming, I was crying, he was spitting on me, calling me an ugly name that begins with C! I got up and he pinned me to the door by my throat, my daughter still in my arms, he let me go. I went to use my phone and he grabbed it and smashed it. How I wish I'd phoned the Police there and then but I didn't, I froze, I didn't know what to do, so I told Ben*, he had to leave. He started looking for somewhere but wouldn't move out. By chance about a month later I phoned the police distraught, I wanted to make sure I could lock him out of my house. The police made a visit. I told them a few things but not much, that was the turning point. I had to go in and make a statement. I made my statement about all the abuse and was then told they would have to arrest him. At this point I was crying and screaming that he would kill me if he knew I had gone to the police. They said he wouldn't be allowed back to the house, they had enough to charge him. He was arrested and charged with 2 counts of assault and 1 count of criminal damage. He was bailed to another address and wasn't allowed to come near me. Needless to say, I still wasn't eating, just drinking. I spent days just crying, shaking and feeling sick, asking myself what had I done.

I had support from my doctor, as well as a domestic abuse charity, who changed my locks and fitted alarms on the windows. They also provided me with counselling and support. They arranged legal advice and I was appointed a solicitor, who was my legal representative when I had to go to court.

I heard that Ben* wanted me to drop the charges, but I wouldn't, I wasn't prepared to have gone through all the work I had done to drop the charges, I wanted him to know that he couldn't treat people this way. We went to court in March 2011, I gave my evidence against him, it was awful. It was such an emotional experience. I had extra measures put in place as in having a screen around him so I couldn't see him. I left the courtroom after giving my evidence. He was found not guilty as it was my word against his. This didn't bother me as such because I wanted him to know he couldn't treat me or anyone that way and to leave me alone.

There was debt on the house that he had built up and the mortgage was in arrears. I spent many hours crying on the phone to debt collection agents telling them what had happened. Due to the debt and because I wasn't working at the time, and couldn't repay the mortgage, I went to the repossession hearing and was told the house would be repossessed and that we were going to be made homeless! I had to register on the council website and bid on a house. I was only allowed to bid once. I was classed as technically homeless, which was the last month before the due eviction. I was lucky, with just days to go before eviction, a house came up in the area. I was still drinking and hardly eating, I had lost a lot of weight.

November 2011, we moved into our new house and things started to look good. My son, daughter and I had a lovely little Christmas. I realised that I was very lucky and that this was our time to shine. I started eating, put weight on, enjoyed life, although I was going through a lot of therapy to get me back to being me. It took me a good 18 months to rebuild myself and feel some semblance of normality.

Even now 13 years on there is still healing to be done around what happened to me. It is more a case of severing all emotional ties that have lingered, so I'm using therapy to sever them.

From the time I met Ben* I endured mental, physical and financial abuse, but I ignored the signs because I believed he loved me and that I could change him! He would punch me, kick me, hit me. Each time he would say 'look what you made me do, this is your fault!' He would steal money off me, stay out all night with other women, yet I still took him back every time. I allowed him to treat me however he wanted because all along I thought I could change him. I would be the one who would turn him into the man he wanted to be.

All this took its toll on me and I was drinking heavily to deal with the situation. I was eating rubbish and started putting weight on. He told me I was ugly, that no one would want me, I was worthless, and I believed him. I don't believe him now, he's a pathological liar.

I want to finish on quoting him when we first split up, he said to me 'when I'm living in my 4 bedroom detached house, I don't want you turning up asking me to take you back!' My reply was 'don't worry I won't'. How the tables have turned, as I finish typing this, sitting at my laptop in my office, in my 4 bedroom detached house!

One thing that comes up a lot is feelings of shame, I feel

it a lot and I know many if not all survivors do. I feel it when I talk about the abuse. I get a sense of people thinking 'well why didn't you just leave after the first time'. Unless you've been there you won't understand. It's not that easy, especially when you're told on countless occasions 'it is all your fault!' You love that person and want to be with them hoping day after day that things will change. What I'm trying to say is, there is no shame, it is NOT your fault!!

**

Michelle Smith is a Counsellor in Training and mum to 3 humans and a dog! A newly evolving Psychic Medium and Angelic Reiki Healer, passionate about her own personal growth and that of others. Michelle firmly sees her life experiences, of which she's had many, as being positive experiences. Which allows her to walk beside survivors of trauma, providing a guiding hand to a place of safety.
https://www.facebook.com/mlsinclair1

Unleashing Your Potential: Connecting, Communicating, And Igniting Change From Within!

Hayley Su Buchanan

This is what I'm going to talk about, Connection. Connection with ourselves. I am the master of the magical morning routine. And mastering it allows us this life experience that we are here living. And if we didn't have these gorgeous bodies, we wouldn't be here, right? So, my son says to me, 'well, duh Mom', and I said, 'yes, but how many times do you forget that your body is the one that is experiencing this life? And do you treat your body like your best friend or your worst enemy? '.

So, who has a high fibre fast internet connection at home?

Do you have that same connection with your body? Is it fast? Do you get what she's saying to you? When she's giving you messages, do you listen or does she have to scream at you to make you stop to go, 'ah, that's not what I want right now'.

Two years ago in June 2021, we emigrated to the UK from South Africa. And in January 2022, I found myself in a very dark place. I have always been uplifting, and inspiring, seeing all the possibilities there are in the world kinda girl. I see the good in everything. But suddenly I was lost, and I thought, what on earth is going on? Why, why can't I get myself out of this? When you're a healer, when you have all the tools, all the techniques to help yourself, and you're in this dark space, yet you can't seem to engage those tools until you are absolutely ready. I couldn't get out of bed. I have two children, and I have a husband, but my husband works away. So, he wasn't even there to support me. And I thought, oh, I have to do something. What am I going to do?

Enter the morning routine. I always had a morning routine, but suddenly because I had become so lost in my emigration process in making sure my kids were okay and making sure that this was okay, and that was okay, I had forgotten about myself. I had forgotten about my body. And my needs. So, I thought, okay, all I can do is give myself three things to do every morning. That's all I can do. Because when you're in a dark space, you can't always do a lot to help yourself, right? So, what were those three things? And this is where connection comes in. Connection is key. Because when you are connected with yourself, you are able to communicate, communicate better with yourself, with your loved ones, with your business partners, with everybody, right?

And that allows for the change. So, these are my three words that I love; connect, communicate, and change. The connection starts before your eyes even open. In the morning, I have taught myself to kind of awaken before my alarm. And what I do is connect with the outside world. What does that look like? It just means I listen. You've been sleeping for five to nine hours, (nine hours sleeper over here) and your body needs time to wake up, slowly, gently come back into this beautiful space. So, I invite you to try these things and see how they work for you. So just listen, are there birds? Is there traffic? Is there somebody walking outside? Is your partner snoring next to you? Just gently allowing those senses to become aroused back into this world.

And then the second thing I do is connect with me, my body, the inner world. And how do I do that? Treat me like my best friend. Ask her how she is feeling, Hey body, good morning. Hug me maybe. And just say thank you. Thank you for waking up this morning. Have gratitude, gratitude for my body for everything that she was yesterday and everything that she will be today. If you don't have a connection with yourself, you cannot connect with anybody else. You cannot move through life disconnected, buffering, waiting for that connection. Do you remember the dial-up modem? Some of us are in that stage of interrupted connection with our bodies.

Uh, uh, uh, am I gonna, uh, uh, am I listening? So, it's just checking in, doing a body scan, going, how are you feeling today? Body, where's the intensity? Where is there resistance? Where am I not being flexible? What nourishment do I want today? What nurturing do you require today? Beautiful body. And I hear you, saying to me, Hayley, I don't have time. I don't have time for this nonsense in the morning, life happens. But you can train yourself to do this in 10 minutes before your alarm has even gone off. And I promise you, when you start to win the morning, you win the day. And when you win the day, you win the week. And when you win the week, you win the month, and so on and so on and so on and so on. And you're winning at life, right? Starting your day in the most beautiful way can only allow you to have a beautiful day. Yes, you may have ups and downs, but you have that space that you've been in that allows you to react in a different way than you would have. That's what it's done for me. I lost myself and I was flying off the handle for everything. Now I know, it's not really worth overreacting about. So, checking in with yourself, asking your body what else is possible. How does it get any better than this? Show me body, show me what else is available for me today.

Now I know your next thought is well, Hayley, how do I know how to listen to my body? An easy way is to stand up, soften your knees, take a deep breath in and relax and say, hey body, am I female/male? Does she move forward, or does he move forward or backward or sideways? Those are little messages from your body. That is your YES from your body. If you haven't connected with your body in this way before, this is a very easy way to start. You can ask your body anything, right? Because when you are asking your body what she wants to eat, you will start to eat in a way that is good for you, not what somebody else is telling you to do because you are different from me. So, what I'm eating may not be what you are meant to eat. What do you want to wear? Body? Do you stand in front of your cupboard and does something, jump out and say, yes, I wanna wear that? And you go, Really? Body. Really? You wanna wear that? And I talk about my body as if she is a different entity to me because she has her own energy. She is separate, but one and the same to me.

So, who's gonna start asking their bodies questions? It's a little bit bizarre, right? I'm a little bit crazy, I'm told all the time, but it's okay. It works for me.

After I've checked in with my body, gone all the way to my beautiful feet, and said, thank you body for allowing me to stand on you for eight to ten hours a day, I then move into affirmations.

I trust myself. I love myself. I am brilliant. I am bright. I am a radiant being of light. Find those affirmations that inspire and uplift you and say them every day. It changes my entire day. It has changed my children's day.

Side note, my son was diagnosed when he was 10 years old, (He's going to be 16 now) with all sorts of learning disabilities, ADHD and dyslexic tendencies. And I was like, oh my God, what am I going to do? After freaking out and looking outside myself, I realised I'd been training for this moment all my life. I could help him. So, I put together a program for him that included visualisations, affirmations, vision boards, and body healing sessions. We did this 3-x week for 6 weeks.

Within six weeks, the teacher said to me, 'did you put him on medication? It was a good call. He's a changed child', I said, 'Hmm, no I did not. He's just been doing the work himself. And now he knows how to help himself'. So those affirmations are so powerful. And eventually, he had his friends saying those affirmations on every test they took, he had taught them to write what percentage they wanted to get for that test. And it's just amazing. It's so inspiring to watch him be empowered.

Step 1 is to connect to your outside world.

Step 2 connect to your inner world, body scan.

Step 3 is affirmations.

Step 4 is pulling energy.

Step 5 is movement.

Everything is energy, right? Everything, you, me, the chair, everything is energy. So, pulling energy through your body just allows stuff to move. Moving allows the energy within your body to move emotions, to flow through and out of your body. Because we are like psychic Sponge Bobs that walk around in the world going, oh, I can feel this. I can feel this, I can feel this. Is it yours to process? Not always. If you just close your eyes right now and ask for energy to flow, it will. Just see it, drop your barriers. Now push those barriers down and just allow that energy to flow up through your feet, pulling it from all directions coming up into your feet, into your legs, through your thighs, your hips, your belly, your heart, your throat, up and out through your head. And just allow that continuous flow of light to move through your body. Feel your cells start to vibrate, start to move, and re-energise. 10 minutes of pulling energy is like taking a three-hour nap.

It invigorates your body, it inspires your body, it calms your body. And then you can reverse that energy and allow it to come down through your head, through your neck and shoulders, down and out through your fingertips, down through your heart, your belly, your hips, your legs, and out through your feet like a shower of light flowing over and through you just gifting to your body. This amazing energy that is abundant, that surrounds us, that is always available to us. And once you've been pulling energy for a while, when your body has had enough, you can get up and move. I normally go and make a cup of tea and then perhaps get the kids up and then I will do my movement for the day, if that's a walk or if that's putting music on, dancing, whatever you choose. These five things are what I do every single morning.

Why would you do any of this? If you have found yourself in a place of darkness, a place where you don't feel like you can anymore, these steps will help you evolve. They will change the energy of your mindset, the energy in your body, and the energy of your life! This won't happen in one day, but being consistent and practicing this routine will make it a habit that you can't live without. And your life will become more magical, more abundant, and definitely more joyful.

I have been sharing this routine with others every day for a year now, and the life changes have been incredible to watch for everyone in the group.

Connect. Communicate. Change.

Connect with your body to allow the communication to flow more easily which creates the change within you that you have been asking for in your world.

Will you try it?

***

Hayley Su Buchanan is a South African native born in Cape Town and currently residing in the UK. A self-proclaimed seeker, she is driven to find more joy, laughter, and success, fuelled perhaps by her mother's influence and a deep-rooted belief in the possibilities of life. Her journey into the energy world began at 17 with Reiki, leading her to explore various modalities like Crystal healing, Enneagram, Mind Power, Body Talk and Chakra healing. Alongside her studies in Hotel Management, she found her passion in healing and intuition development. After her son's learning disabilities diagnosis, she honed her skills to help others unleash their full potential, using energy and mindset techniques she mastered over 25 years. Emphasising the power of energy, Hayley encourages individuals to harness positive thoughts and create the reality they desire. With her unique blend of physical and energetic knowledge, she helps people overcome obstacles and achieve their dreams. Start the day with a positive routine, she advises, for what we focus on shapes our reality and attracts all that life has to offer.

Heal@hayleysubuchanan.com

@hayley_su

Rise From The Ashes Into Your Imperfect Masterpiece

Kelisha Taylor

In this chapter I want to share my personal journey of experiencing domestic abuse, the steps I took to overcome my struggles that can be used in any part of your life and show you what is possible when you find self love and rise from the ashes into your imperfectly perfect masterpiece.

14 years ago, I met a man who I believed was the love of my life. I was only 19 and he was 15 years older than me. Like any relationship the first few months were so beautiful, everything was good as most relationships are. We spent a lot of time together. I absolutely was in love with him, all I could see was the happy ever after that every girl dreamed about when they were a child.

Things changed quickly when I became pregnant with our first child. He went from sweet and charming to disrespectful and belittling, making me feel worthless and dirty. Cheating became his new hobby. He accused me of our son not being his or looking like him. I was always told I didn't have any sense and that I was an idiot. Verbal abuse became the new norm in life especially when he couldn't get what he wanted.

My first experience of physical violence was being smacked in the face and him grabbing a hammer almost hitting me with it. I realised that he was trying to scare me, still thankful though as it could have been a lot worse! Things never got better though, it got worse. I tried to see the good in him and believed one day he would change. The control of who I could talk to and where I could go was getting out of control, but I listened to him.

I remember the one time being timed to get back from a mutual friend's house who lived just around the corner from his mum's house. It was tipping down with rain. I grabbed our child and hurried back. When I got to his mum's house, he was already outside waiting for me, eyes bloodshot! He asked me what took me so long, and when he speaks I must listen. He was very good at cursing me out quietly without being heard. He took our son inside the house and dragged me around the side of the house and started shouting at me. That is when he punched me in my belly so hard I dropped to the floor. I couldn't breathe, I couldn't speak. I was crying and shaking uncontrollably. He flipped out his knife and went to use it but his mum appeared and cried out asking what was going on. He put the knife away quickly before his mum could see it and told her it was a disagreement, and everything was ok.

Unknowingly, I was pregnant at this time, which I found out two days later. Sadly that ended in a miscarriage, losing what would have been our second child. When I told him I was pregnant and I had lost it, he insulted me by telling me

I was a walking graveyard, I couldn't even carry his child, making me feel so crappy about myself and believing it was my fault.

He did things discreetly. No one would ever have known. But despite the abuse, I stayed with him as I was in love and believed he would change, and I believed him when he said he was sorry and it wouldn't happen again.

Eventually, after 4 years, I couldn't take anymore and that is when I left, sent a text to him and locked my door. However, I was 23 years old, and because of co-dependency issues, I entered into another relationship very soon, within weeks with someone else.

This time I became the abuser. I was verbally abusive, bitter, angry, depressed, an emotional wreck, filled with anxiety, rebellious, lacked self-love and care for myself. I was filled with self-doubt, needy as hell, always stuck in my own head, mentally and energetically drained, and lost my identity – you name it, I was all this except physically violent towards him. I became the worst mother ever.

My turning point was when depression started getting the best of me. I struggled to run my business, be a mum, and be a partner. My life wasn't 'normal' and even though I wasn't together with my ex he still had control over me. I could feel it, plus there was a part of me that loved him and couldn't understand after all the love I had given him why would he do this to me. I never got an answer before I left him, so I was always left questioning – why?

It took me 5 rough years to heal from the bitter and hurt person I had become and that is what I want to share with you.

Things changed for me when I found spirituality and learned about the importance of self-love and self-care. I learned how to face my past, heal my present, and not only forgive myself but also forgive him, the person who had put me through so much pain. He had his own inner wounds he had inflicted on me and he also still needed to heal. But the most important thing I learned was how to find myself and truly love myself unconditionally. I know the Universe never wanted me to keep what I have learned through this experience a secret, so I am sharing with you the unknowing journey I was on and I hope that it can help guide and inspire someone out there.

There were 4 steps I was guided on without even knowing I was on that journey. The journey of S.E.L.F. It was time to become more selfish with my love and with myself and it wasn't until I had the download that was through S.E.L.F, that I found my peace again. Let me explain what S.E.L.F means when you break it down.

I want you to take a deep breath and close your eyes – didn't that feel nice to just reset and ground?

THE FIRST STEP IS TO SURRENDER.

I learnt that surrendering was the land of the dead. It's a place where you have to let go of everything you feel – bitterness, anger, fear, worry, you name it. Does it happen overnight? Hell no, as a matter of fact every time you let something go something else comes up. It was like opening an ants nest for me, and everything came to the surface. More hurt, overwhelm, emotions. The point of surrendering is letting go of the bull in order to rise. This is sweeping the ashes into a pile and wondering what to do with it next.

THE NEXT STEP IS TO EVALUATE.

No matter what happens in your life in order to grow you

need to be willing to stop, look, understand, and see what is what. Once you have surrendered to what you have been holding onto, then is the time you need to look at each piece of the puzzle. Understanding the who, what, where, when, and why, and a lot of us don't like looking back and understanding because it brings us more hurt but sis let me tell you this, it's through the storm you find divine clarity.

THE NEXT STEP IS TO LOVE.

This isn't easy for some but a phase of compassion, love, forgiveness – not only to yourself but to others who have done you wrong. Now because you have forgiven them it doesn't mean you are going to open your arms and say "hey I am here lets be friends again so you can shit on me." All you are simply saying is love heals and conquers and brings you peace. Through love you learn, you become a clear energetical match to not only heal your wounds but learn who you are destined to be – birth your true brilliance into existence.

THE FINAL STEP IS TO FOCUS.

This is where you have taken all you have learned and start to build a healthier life than what you knew. It's about setting a holistic approach to how you live your life, becoming who you are, living life on your terms, setting goals and plans that keep you aligned and true to who you are, on your terms. Standing at the other end with your peace, and clarity. Looking at yourself as once ashes, imperfectly put back together with even more value, becoming a rebel masterpiece, a valuable piece of art because no one can do what you did – you've walked the valley of the shadow of death and come out the other side.

MY MESSAGE TO YOU.

When a woman feels she is so broken and she thinks she hasn't got the strength to get up and rise again, I tell women, even your ashes can be turned back into your masterpiece, you can get up again.

This is your time to rise, this is your time to become. This is your time to express your beautiful true rebel brilliance in a light and fashion without fear, without oppression and suppression. You are so destined to be more and do more. Your day will come when YOU will be the changemaker in someone else's life because we all need you.

You are beautiful, unique and special just as you were designed to be by the universe, and I want you to stand up, grab those boobies and tell yourself, I am doing it all for me, this is my time to shine, this is my time to thrive!

You have lived your life for far too long being an empathic lover to all. Energy vampires see it, they know it, and they will suck and pull your last being if they can have enough not to find another victim to feed off. This is your time to start getting to grips with that thing called selfish love! What does that look like? Knowing what you will and won't put up with, telling the world to sod off without guilt if it doesn't make you feel happy, boundaries are a girl's new best friend. If you haven't got to meet her yet you are missing a trick. Having self care without guilt, knowing you deserve it and are worthy of it, that is selfish self love in a nutshell.

Now, I am on a mission to inspire and empower other women who have faced adversity on why it's important to heal through self-love. It's non-negotiable, especially if you want a loving relationship with your children, partner, and others. Every woman needs to have a deep self-connection before she can love anyone else or live a 'normal' life. I want to see more women take back their powers, know and love themselves unconditionally and turn their pain into their powers that let them live a life of purpose, and never having to conform to anyone else again. I want to see more women speaking their truth and walking in their beautiful rebel brilliance.

I am here to remind you beautiful souls that it's not easy, but you survived the storm so your truth could get told. You are worthy of happiness, joy, peace, freedom, and ALL you desire. I am here to let you know you are not alone and so many women like you are trying to rise and now is the time for your happy ending – the next chapter of your life is waiting to be written.

I wish you nothing but the best and success.

***

Hey, I am Kelisha Taylor, I am a self love and wellness mentor, a rebel empowerment speaker, an intuitive spiritual guide and a survivor of domestic abuse. When I am not saving the world, I am a homeschooling mama to 5 humans and obsessed with all things to do with spiritual/personal development, self love to better self. I am very down to earth, very practical and analytical in the way I guide others with a no fucks given type of energy, keeping things real and transparent.

I also want to thank the universe that I am able to be a part of a collective set of powerful women able to spread love and light and healing into the world.

www.facebook.com/Kelisha.Taylor.1

BE YOU

Keri Denney

Be the best you that you can be.

Had I learned this earlier in my life I think things would have been different.

I am a great believer in you live your life, and all those experiences shape who you are, but had I known that being me was enough, I would have made different choices. I would have celebrated my own personal victories. I would have celebrated my uniqueness, my quirks, and desires sooner. I would not have wasted so much time and energy doing stuff that was not in alignment with me, my soul, and my purpose.

There are definitely highlights in my life so far that break the mould, ways that I did life differently, but I also kept myself small, and maybe still do.

My schooling looked normal. I took the classes I was supposed to, did what was asked, attempted to play an instrument, and did other activities that were available. I had fun, mostly, but I never asked myself if I was really interested in any of this. What was I interested in doing?

My husband and child are very clear on what they are interested in, what they want to do, and most importantly what they will not do. I get confused sometimes and then I rest easy knowing that they are solid in themselves. They know what they want, and they have no problem saying it. You always know where you stand with them. I love this about them. Especially since we can talk about anything with each other.

I did not know it was ok to ask questions. I did not know that it was ok to not know what you did not know. One time in primary school, that always stands out for me, was in maths class.

I did not already know how to do these particular maths problems and I could not bring myself to ask for help. I felt embarrassed. I felt shame. I felt stupid. I just let the allotted time get away from me. When the teacher asked us to hand in our paper, I burst out in tears. Tears! Inconsolable tears, over maths! I took some time outside and got a hold of myself but at 10 or so years old I did not know why I felt the way I did or what I could do about it.

Figuring nobody liked me or would be interested in dating me I never trusted my instincts on the right person to date or my feelings towards men. I believed if you acted right and you did certain things right then someone would ask you out. But that does not put you in your own personal power and really expressing yourself and (I know now) attracting the right person.

Needless to say, I attracted a lot of duds that did not work out. I blamed them, I tore myself down, and I dropped my expectations. I made many bad choices. I tore myself down more and dropped my expectations again because this must be my fault. I did not know what I did not know. That same hurt, shame, and embarrassment from the maths problems still burned fresh in my belly.

Remember, if you are pretending to be something you are not, you are going to attract someone who wants a pretend version of you. You have trapped yourself in a box of your own making.

This erodes your own understanding of who you are, you forget what lights you up and you keep expecting less and less and less.

I felt like the "dating me" was a watered-down version of the whole me.

I thought perhaps I could express myself fully somewhere else, express myself with my closest friends only. Maybe expressing myself wasn't that important. I am sure there are many people in the world that have no idea what it is to be happy. To be themselves. That's ok…right? But wait, life is meant to be lived to the fullest. To be happy or at least do your best each day to be happy and enjoy your time here. I am not talking about toxic, paint a fake smile on your face, look now I am happy. I mean deep in your soul, truly content with your life, your choices, your dreams, who you spend your time with, and how you inspire others without realising it. Allowing the light within you to shine so bright that it fuels your daily purpose. Whatever that may be. Express yourself and your creativity. As long as you are not hurting anyone, including yourself, then embrace the choices that make sense for you. Not everyone thinks like you. Maths may come very easily to you (like my kid) and you breeze through easily. Working in an office Monday to Friday was not good for me, for my overall wellness in life. Could I do it? Yes. But was there a better way? Yes.

I found my Massage Therapy career this way and felt

guided to add in essential oils which have enhanced my health and creativity, plus increased my effectiveness with my clients, and I continue teaching them how to use essential oils in their own self care. I also went after my dream of teaching Zumba fitness. It is so much fun and brings so much joy to me and my community.

Even though I spent a lot of time with the wrong people it was not all wasted. I learned so much about myself, gradually.

Had I known that being fully me was enough I would not have wasted so much time being destructive to myself.

Each time I said yes because they asked. Each time I didn't speak up when I should have. Each time I should have said no. I learned. I learned to speak up for myself. I learned how to recognise I was just going along. I learned to advocate for my needs. I never wanted to give up on any relationship, loyal to a fault some may say. I eventually realised I would rather be alone than continue dating or living with someone because it was logical.

But if things are not working, if day in and day out there is more stress than joy, if communication and mutual understanding are not an active part of the journey, then realise you can actually move on and it is ok. I would be ok. I could learn from my experiences as can you.

I became more aware of my intuition, that inner voice we all have but often ignore because we are told we are being silly or it is not logical. Where is your proof? I learned how my intuition felt when it was communicating with me. I learned how it felt when I listened to my intuition. I learned that nobody could take that away from me when I made a decision that I knew was guided by my intuition, that felt right instead of just going along because I was supposed to say yes to be good, or not to make waves.

I was ok with being me, I am enough.

If I had a partner, that would be a bonus but my expectations of who I would share my life, my time and my energy with was very specific. I would no longer sacrifice my energy for just anyone.

The Universe heard me because I met the love of my life in a seemingly magical way. We continue to love each other unconditionally every day. We communicate our needs and wishes as they arise. We discuss problems and misunderstandings as they come up. We accept each other exactly how we are. Sometimes, I fall back into old habits of not listening to the words being spoken and hear through a filter of I have done something wrong...something I should have known already, but how? Wait, what was actually said? I ask my partner to hold on, back up or repeat so I can listen with new ears and get back on track, without an old grimy filter. This takes practice and commitment. I want to communicate, understand and grow. If I jump into a destructive pattern this will just stunt open, honest, communication. I believe communication is our greatest tool in any and all relationships. Remembering this helps me to be a better mother, wife, friend, daughter, and business owner. Did we break the mould? Maybe a little bit. He asked me to marry him after 7 weeks of dating. We were married less than a year after our first date. I had always wanted to move to Ireland (but that is not what you do) and he loved our visits to Ireland and we decided together that we could make it happen. So, we did.

I went to school as expected and went to a few junior Colleges (this is a mid-way step in the USA after high school and before University). I have my degree in nothing much, and headed into the workforce. This is how you are supposed to do it, right? During this time I dabbled in different jobs and took a variety of classes like sign language, drama, improv, fitness and ceramics. During this time I discovered that there are different ways to learn. Visual, Auditory and Kinesthetic. Everything I learned that was hands-on sunk in faster and easier versus years of lectures or texts that I did not absorb. I was having fun while learning in my 20s. I was asking questions and releasing any shame or embarrassment of not knowing. I was there to learn. I can only do that by asking questions. I kept reminding myself, like an affirmation or mantra, I do not know what I do not know. Wow, what if I knew about hands-on learning in my early years of schooling, how much stress and doubt could have been avoided? All this time I figured I was not good at school and I must not be very smart.

I started an office job full time at a good company doing customer service. I loved helping people, troubleshooting problems and learning new skills. But the day to day office worker mentality had me stressed and ageing prematurely. I did not smile as much. If you have met me you know this is a huge indicator of how things were going on inside of me. I fell into a Monday to Friday work routine. Then I went out drinking and making bad decisions on the weekends. Hate Mondays. Repeat. For 3 years. The Universe had planted seeds of random encounters with folks doing life differently over these 3 years. So when the stress was too much I reached out to Massage Therapy schools in my area, and just thought I would consider doing something different because this Monday to Friday office stress could not be all there is to a career and adulthood. I visited one Massage school, quit my job and became a Massage Therapist. On the first day of school I was exactly where I needed to be. I was so calm and sure of my choice I knew my intuition had guided me. When I think back I can still feel that knowing sense. I was enough. I can learn in ways that work for me. I can have a career that I enjoyed. My life choices are up to me. I can be me. I can ask questions. I can get answers. I can question my own thoughts and understanding. I can do all this without shame.

If you are waiting for permission to be you, like I often do, here it is: Be you. This won't happen all at once but with each choice, with each boundary, with each experience, you will be more you. Express all that you are, because that is what we need more of in this world.

Imagine if every person used their energy and talents for the good of all people. Imagine all the possibilities and innovation. The strength of community. Imagine being happy with your day to day living. This could be reaching for the stars or keeping up with housework. Your life, your goals, your choices.

You are enough.

Be You.

***

Keri Denney grew up in California and is now living in Ireland, happily ever after with her husband and child. She is delighted to be included in this book with her chapter 'Be You'.

Keri is all about helping people feel fabulous. She is a Massage Therapist, Wellness Advocate, and Zumba Fitness Instructor. Keri has learned so much about herself by working with other people on their wellness journeys. Keri is here to support you as well, wherever you are on your path. 'I hope my experience will inspire you to shine bright, I am so grateful for all the time, energy and experience that has been poured into this book'.

http://www.keridenneywellness.ie/

Revelations Of A Betrayed Heart

Nikki Pinto

My name is Nikki, I am a survivor of abuse and I'm passionate about supporting survivors. It's important to me that I can raise awareness about what abuse looks like and prevent it from happening, as there is much work to be done in this area.

I'm so thankful to God as I have been abundantly blessed, I would not be the creative person I am today if it wasn't for the shit I've had to go through, it has made me tenacious and strong. I have amazing friends and a partner who I love and I know he loves and supports me unconditionally.

In retrospect, it was obvious the previous relationship was doomed from the start. I had no idea what 'gaslighting' was, I'd never heard of 'love-bombing', there were so many 'red flags' in the first few weeks, but I ignored them. His insane jealousy scared me, the endless texting distracted me, the proclamations of love, the showering of flowers and gifts, and the little notes of affirmation all boosted my fragile ego to the point of submission, I was bombarded and literally swept off my feet.

Hindsight is a wonderful thing, looking back the creepiest part of it all was his patience, he waited a year before he made his move. I gave him all the cards; he knew everything about me and I knew nothing of him. We worked at the same place. He was a night worker. I was a manager on shifts so I got to spend time with the night staff. I never really noticed him, he was always in the background, he didn't say much, we never got friendly and he certainly wasn't my 'type', I was married anyway.

I invited the night workers out to watch the Euro final, I wasn't particularly interested in football but the staff were all men so it was stereotypically appropriate. I spotted him walking across the road. It was clear he had made an effort with his attire, and his overpowering fragrance arrived before him. He was smiling like a Cheshire cat as he waddled towards me, he told me the other staff had things on so it was just us, this was the first red flag I ignored. I was disappointed as I was friendly with the other staff, however, we headed into town. By the end of the night, we were both drunk and his confidence grew. As we walked to work, where I was staying, he tried to kiss me. I was very firm and told him "NO", I was married and he replied with a shrug of his shoulders, "Technically so am I". I was surprised at how flippant he was about marriage, the next red flag ignored, I knew he was going through a separation so assumed he was apathetic towards marriage, which was odd given that two weeks into our relationship he asked me to marry him, another red flag ignored.

It wasn't long before I found myself separating from my then-husband, whom I had been with for 11 years. We were very good friends, more like brother and sister than husband and wife. Our separation was amicable, my husband went to live in Spain while my head was getting seduced by 'him', and I found myself in an intense and volatile relationship. I became isolated from friends because of his jealousy. He did not like me being near anyone else, male, or female, relations, colleagues, or friends. I became uncomfortable going out, so I stopped to please him, as somehow, he had beguiled my loyalty like a spell had been put on me.

Our first 'date' was a disaster, he got drunk and played pool for most of the night so I chatted with his friends and family. Before I knew it, I was up against a wall in a neck lock with him accusing me of flirting, it all transpired so fast I was terrified, I reinforced I was not flirting. Once he released his grip, I ran to get my coat and bag and left the building, however, I was in the middle of an estate and lost. I called his son who met me, his eldest warned me about 'him', and told me 'he' had always been more interested in women and drinking than his five other children, more red flags. The next day I went to stay with a friend who was very supportive, I swore that I would never have anything to do with him, however, he bombarded me with apologetic texts and I ended up forgiving the incident, putting it down to the alcohol, it was the first time I tried to finish with him.

When I sold our marital home, my husband came back from Spain to help clear it. During this time, I had to end the relationship with 'him' again because he became so manipulative and jealous. I couldn't cope with the stress after he threatened suicide and tried to intimidate my husband for staying in the same house as me, even though we were joint owners! Splitting from 'him' was quite a relief, I got a new job, a nice flat and my life was going well, then one day he sent a text message, I should have ignored it but I didn't and it was not long before I was back with him, the biggest mistake I made.

He love-bombed me, my house was like a florist's, he idolised me, showered me with affection, gestures, and gifts. He made me promises, broke them, then gaslit me. I gave him ammunition to manipulate my psyche; he went from venerating me to devaluing me on a regular basis to the point I did not know what reality looked like. It was his way or nothing, no compromise.

I eventually declared our relationship at work. It turned out that because I was a manager, I was in breach of company policy. He kept his job and refused to find another when I had to leave. I stupidly had an expectation he would show some loyalty to me, but he didn't, more red flags I ignored.

It took a year before I finally moved in with him. He regularly asked me but I refused. One day I went to open my front door but I couldn't get out because it had been stuck to the door frame from the outside with Duct Tape, the word 'Paki' was stuck on the door. I did not tell many people how I was bullied at school because of my skin colour but I told him, he knew the word 'Paki' would trigger fear into me. I was scared so I called him, he put it into my head that the neighbours did it, there was no mention of calling the police, he insisted I should live with him so he could keep me safe, I felt vulnerable as I was six months pregnant, so I reluctantly agreed to move in with him. Two days later I was packed up and ready to leave. His sister and her husband drove the van, and when we set off, he wrote me a note, "Now I've got you I will never let you go." It freaked me out a bit but I just smiled at him, inside I was questioning, "What am I doing?"

Two weeks later he smashed all the things that were dear to me. Once he told me I was too much of a free spirit and he would have to clip my wings. I let him depersonalise me because I was scared of being on my own as I was pregnant.

He was a prolific liar and would lie over the smallest thing, then when challenged he got the chance to cause an argument. The number of times I split up with him over the 12 years actually became a joke with his family, my mother, and the one friend I was allowed to have, who turned out to be his 'flying monkey', (a person used to manipulate and send and give messages). I even lived in a refuge when my son was 2 months old and still, I went back, I became his yo-yo. He had total control of my emotions, my confidence was shattered, and I was his 'scapegoat', an emotional punch bag for him and I had no idea.

In year seven he started having affairs. By this time, I was codependent, (emotionally locked in a life with him), and I trusted him implicitly. At the start of our relationship, he told me of two people who had cheated on him. He reinforced that he would never cheat because he knew what it felt like, and I believed him. I got suspicious about one woman fairly quickly but chose to ignore my instinct thinking I was paranoid. After three months of suspicion, on my birthday, I waited for him to go to sleep. I took his phone which was hidden in a neatly folded pile of clothes, (he guarded his phone even though he checked my phone and internet searches regularly) after much digging I found some evidence of two women he was fucking. It took two weeks of hard-core lying and gaslighting (he made me think it was all in my head), before he finally admitted, on Valentine's Day, that he had slept with one of them. This sent me into the start of a nervous breakdown, he just packed his things and called his sister to pick him up. There was no conversation about it, I was not allowed to get angry, I did lash out at him and he just left. After a week of being ghosted (no contact) with my son and me I got in touch because I wanted to sort out child contact arrangements. Somehow the next day he was back living in our house, I was not allowed to talk about the affairs, and when I did, which was often, it turned into an argument. After a few weeks of stress, I told him to leave again, the ghosting happened again then I discovered he had got with a third woman. He ignored his responsibilities as a father until I again got in touch with him to have some contact with his son. I should have known better as he had five other children who he did not give a shit about so why should my child be any different?

It only took a month for him to get back into my life again, his arm was covered in a tasteless tattoo of roses and skulls with the words Mum and Dad scrolled into the design. Just after his mother died, he started the affairs, so I put them down to bereavement or depression. He was a Mummy's boy; she created the monster. I went back to work early after maternity leave because I could not stand her coming to our house every day and hiding anything that was out of place, including my son's toys, so our house looked tidy. She was a troublemaker within the family, she had obvious favourite children, he was her best boy, she infantilised him and he loved being looked after by her. I was relieved when she was put into a home when dementia kicked in, he showed no real emotion about it, even when she died.

When he came home this time with a pile of debt, I ended up paying it off and consolidated the loans we had already had because he spent most of our wages, I never did find out on what. When he left, he stopped paying for the loan, which was in my name, I was left with £23k of debt. The bank was really helpful because I could prove coercive control, they wrote the debt off for me.

As a result of my breakdown, I started to get productive and began a creative journey. I opened a website, Something Out Of Nothing, which exhibits my artwork and Anti-Fashion and I sold paintings on eBay. What with my job, which was demanding and took me away overnight a lot, my creativity and his shifts we barely saw each other and when we did, we argued a lot. The last time he put me in a neck lock against a wall my son rugby tackled him off me, this was the beginning of the end for me as I realised how affected my son was getting.

It was mid-October 2015 when I finally did it, I told him our marriage was over and I made him leave. I had no idea what was in store for me, I buried my head in my faith, painting, gardening, decorating, wild camping with my son, and making friends to keep myself busy. On the outside everything may have looked good but in reality, things got worse which is common when a 'supply' leaves the relationship. I read a lot about narcissistic abuse, there was no diagnosis but he ticked a lot of the boxes that constitute narcissism so I familiarised myself with them, to protect myself. I also did a lot of praying because I felt extremely vulnerable, worried about being a single parent and scared of him and his family who turned on both my son and me. My faith and my friends helped me stay strong, though it was hard because his family tried to get my son taken from me and the police didn't help me. Thankfully, I got through it with lots of support from my doctor and my son's school. I updated them and the police on everything that happened so there was a record of events if I needed them. I even managed to divorce him on my own without a solicitor, I made sure the divorce papers stated domestic abuse and infidelity, that was my way of warning other women.

After leaving him I was forced to take a good look at myself in order to figure out why I put up with the relationship for so long. I realised there was an element of familiarity as my childhood had been difficult, treading on eggshells was natural to me, I was accustomed to being put down and bursts of violence were sadly homespun. There seemed to be a generational curse that females in my family were brought up in a very Catholic, strict, abusive way. I'm glad to say I have broken that curse; I had a boy who I cherish and I left the Catholic church!

I participated in Schema Therapy for a while, it really helped me understand the different facets of my personality and Art Therapy gave me the opportunity to bring my 'characters' to life. The therapies provided support for my family too as it is not easy being the child or partner of a survivor of abuse. Personally, I believe there should be support groups for the partners of survivors as it's a challenging journey. A partner who is willing to learn about the anxieties and 'triggers' of survivors will get a truly strong, loyal consort who is capable of a tremendous amount of love if given the chance because love is the key and asking myself every day, "Who am I?"

***

Nikki Pinto studied art, fashion and design for five years at college and has carried on her creative journey as a therapeutic hobby. In between working and looking after her son, she has built up a collection of up-cycled 'Anti-Fashion' and enjoys painting, jewellery making, and anything creative really! Nikki hopes to, one day, set herself up in her business as 'Something Out Of Nothing' selling her 'Anti-Fashion' garments, appendages and art.

Nikki has set up a website www.soon46.co.uk where her collections and artwork can be viewed. 'Ideally, I would love to collaborate with other survivors and bring creatives together under the Something Out Of Nothing banner'.

RECLAMATION

Christine Kenny

I really don't know why I tried so hard to fit in.

I had two main goals in life, one was not to be embarrassed, to hide anything that might cause people to laugh at me, to hide anything that might make people think I am odd or feel sorry for me.

The other was to be heard and understood but not in a way that meant I would stand out!

It's quite complex and not logical at all because it has all developed from stories, conditioning, and traumas.

Where it began, I don't know, but I do know when I became aware that I needed to change it.

It was January just after I turned 47, I wanted to die, I didn't want to kill myself because that would be too awful for my family. I wanted my life to end or get really ill so that people couldn't blame me for being such a failure. I was a failure. I was a failure, and it was not only embarrassing but the guilt completely overwhelmed me.

I remember when the guilt started and the overwhelming drive to prove my existence to everyone began. I was around

30. I had spent a large part of my life trying to prove myself, but this seemed to be the turning point.

I had a loving boyfriend and we had 3 happy children. Everything seemed great on the outside.

But I had lost my identity. I needed to prove that I was capable and that there really was more to me.

I didn't do well at college, I dropped out and went travelling with my boyfriend. I made jewellery at this time, and we sold it as we travelled. After that I had various jobs but nothing I would consider exciting or meaningful.

I never did well at school either, I thought I was dumb. I remember hearing teachers say that I wasn't as clever as my brother. Most of the time I decided that I couldn't do it, so I zoned out and daydreamed instead.

I was told I had neat handwriting and that I was a good girl. That was what I was good at so I held on to that. I loved to get praise, that was a good feeling so I did more of what I got praise for and avoided the things I couldn't do.

I proved to myself enough times that if I tried to push myself with things that I couldn't do, that I would fail and well, it was embarrassing so I learnt to stop trying. If I couldn't understand something I simply shut down, my brain said "No you can't do this" and that was that.

So back to being 30, I was good at cooking, I was fascinated by food and nutrition and I had been as a child. Cooking and baking was the thing I was good at. I like to eat well so it seemed like the logical step to start working in this field. I decided that I wanted to be a nutritionist, so I set off to go back to college then University, then I'd get a meaningful career. Because I had decided that I needed to do something to prove my worth. Not because I had a burning desire, but I needed to prove my worth!

A few years before, I found myself back at 'school' metaphorically, but with a lot more awareness of people. I felt myself constantly having to prove my worth to the women around me. I was trying to fit in with these women who I really didn't have anything in common with other than children of the same age.

I also felt guilty for being a stay at home mum. It meant we were relying on my boyfriend's wage which was enough for us to get by and have nice things, but I felt that I was letting everyone down. I compared myself to these women who were on Maternity leave and had great careers, seemingly having it all, or the other stay at home mums who had affluent lives, it was considered a 'gift' that they could do that, they had careers before and may go back to them.

I did my best to fit in, say the right things but I was excluded. I didn't fit in and I felt it and I overheard it.

If it was just me, I doubt I would have bothered much, because I had learnt to push away unpleasant feelings, but now it wasn't just me. I had children that needed to fit in and not be embarrassed about their mum who has done nothing.

So it began, I first took a Science access course to get on the degree course. Turned out I was good at it, getting a distinction, but someone told me it was really easy and basic, so I thought better of celebrating myself and my achievement.

I managed to get a place at the nearest University which was 40 minutes drive away.

My life revolved around dropping the children off at school, driving to University, picking them up, making dinner, then studying, because I had to pass or I would be a failure!

I was actually doing well but I couldn't take my eye off the ball. I felt so guilty for putting my children in afterschool clubs, I felt so guilty about focusing on my studies, I just felt really selfish. I was supposed to be feeling worthy!

4 years later I graduated with a 2:1 with honours. I didn't celebrate, I moved on to finding work to prove my worth and to pay back the money I spent trying to prove my worth.

Then to work, I escalated in my role quite quickly, but I didn't believe in myself. I kept thinking it was a fluke, that someone would find out how bad I was, and I would be publicly shamed! I really wanted to work with women improving their health, it actually felt easier and less scary, so I decided to set up my own business, 3 months into working.

Within a few weeks I got my first client and then it grew and grew, so I left the clinical role. I had my own nutrition clinic and personal training studio, but then I also got some locum work, just in case I failed and needed a backup!

Fast forward 5 years. I don't really know how many hours I was working back then, I had steady personal training clients, I had nutrition clients, I never turned anyone away or refused early morning or late night requests and also three days a week I was doing a two hour commute for a 'backup' job.

Then the most awful thing happened. My daughter who had been suffering with her mental health told me she wanted to die. I picked her up from University and we went straight to the doctors.

The same day I took my daughter to the hospital, the Pandemic started and we went into lockdown.

The next day my backup job went online and I worked as though nothing had happened. I buried it into my body with everything else and continued to hustle to prove my worthiness.

Don't get me wrong I was with my daughter, she was

broken but she was at home, we were getting help and at the same time I was working as if nothing had ever happened.

Like most people I moved my business online, took more hours at the backup job and hustled, the only way I knew how to prove my worth was to hustle.

I felt incredibly guilty for spending money and time on myself. I didn't see it as improving the finances for the family. I saw it as a selfish act, something I did for me to prove that I wasn't a failure.

12 months later I crashed, I was exhausted and broken. I knew I had to change something, but I really didn't know what. I think I jumped from the frying pan into the fire. I had witnessed so many women making millions online, seemingly overnight. I can do that too, I thought. I am just as capable.

I gave up the 'backup job' to focus on my business and spiralled into debt, trying to prove my worth yet again. I was desperate to bury my guilt and become a success.

9 months later I finally gave in. I gave in because I had nothing left, I had a massive business debt, I was living on credit cards, any money I had made to contribute to our family life went into my business, but I wasn't getting anywhere.

I was paying coach after coach to save me, just so I could finally prove to everyone that I was worthy.

This was my darkest hour, it was then I wanted to die, but it was also my epiphany moment. At rock bottom you can stay or climb and I chose to climb.

It sends shivers down my body when I write that I was 47 years old before I realised that I have nothing to prove, I am capable and worthy just as I am.

Before I maxed out, I had invested in a mindset course and a healing program. In the mindset course I had begun to understand more about the subconscious and realised that I had some major limiting beliefs. I started reading more around this and decided that even though I had a 'great' childhood, maybe there was something I was missing, and the healing might be the missing link in my business journey.

Then the gates opened! I finally allowed myself to feel into the impact of my daughter's depression instead of blocking it out. I finally allowed myself to feel into the impact of 2 years of emotional abuse, stalking and then an attempt to kill me by an ex-boyfriend.

I finally allowed myself to feel into who I am, not who I believed I was supposed to be.

With that freedom, I started to drop the guilt and I started showing up authentically, I meditated, I journaled, and I realised a lot of really good stuff about myself that I had never noticed before.

I started to take action without fear or embarrassment. My life started changing. I was back working locum again without guilt, I suddenly started getting a lot more interest online and my business picked up.

I allowed myself to ask for help with my finances without fear of what people might think about me. I started talking about the debt and it started helping me release guilt, and it was helping other people too.

Then I came across Breathwork. The shifts were already happening, but Breathwork took me to another level completely. I realised that I have always been worthy and that was enough to open my energetic capacity to receive more and more. I was expanding, my business was expanding.

Breathwork takes you deep into your body, not just uncovering limiting beliefs but peeling them away, shattering them and revealing your truth. We go through life disowning parts of us, we push hurt and pain away and with that we push parts of ourselves away.

The VERY parts that make YOU whole, unique and special. Breathwork releases the parts of you that you thought you had to hide, it brings them back so you can reclaim all of you, breathwork eradicates the stories you heard that keep you small.

Breathwork changed my life. Not just because my business blew up, it changed everything, my relationship with my boyfriend, my children and myself.

Did I need to go through everything to come out the other side as the woman I am, I think I did. I don't believe what we go through is a lesson, I believe we have always been who we are but indoctrination, trauma, and conditioning cause us to hide who we are, and by reclaiming our lost and fragmented parts we become more powerful.

I was always meant to be an expansion facilitator, it took me 47 years to discover my gifts and now I am the changemaker for other women, and they go on to change other women's lives.

I'm part of the reclamation of womanhood and I claim that power now.

***

Christine is a trauma informed success facilitator for women in business.

Using her unique blend of intuitive coaching, shadow work, inner child healing and Breathwork. This deeply powerful work is healing and transformative. Closing trauma loops, removing limiting beliefs and inherited trauma, so women can show up authentically, regulated and in their power, becoming an energetic match for success and abundance.

This work was created from Christine's own journey from the darkness of anxiety and debt to creating a life of freedom, through reclaiming her authentic self.

Christine says, "I had lost parts of me in my journey to be seen and accepted. It took burnout to find them again, but my journey back to self, brought so much self acceptance, I believe it had to happen for that very reason. Remembering who we are and being safe in our body to share that with radical self-acceptance is powerful"

It is my honour to share this work today, when women reclaim their voice and walk in radical self acceptance we change the world.

Connect with Christine on Facebook

Find out more about working with Christine Linktree.

From Addiction To Empowerment

Sarah Ibrahim

It doesn't matter who you are, where you've come from, or what you've been through, you ALWAYS have the power to make a decision that will change the trajectory of your life forever.

It takes courage and commitment to make those decisions into lasting changes, but I'm here to tell you that it absolutely can be done and I'm going to show you how.

My own story sees me growing up with deep rooted abandonment issues, which I was wholly unaware of. This manifested as a 20+ year drug addiction which took over my entire adult life until I was 39 years old! Imagine never living a day with a straight head on as an adult and then finally quitting the drugs and suddenly seeing the world through a whole new lens! It looked, and felt, like lost for a long time – but that was an illusion. It was simply a new and exciting world that I never previously knew existed! It was scary AF too because I knew nothing about how to navigate this experience without my trusty little friend, but we'll come on to that in a bit.

What I've come to realise is that cocaine was my stability, I always knew where I was with it. Because of the nature of my party-girl ways, lots of things in my life were fluid. Relationships came and went, money came and went, jobs came and went, my Dad even came and went, but drugs? Well, they were always there for me. A sanctuary where I knew I could escape to and no-one could touch me. It was a special space, just for me.

Pain and suffering didn't exist in this little bubble, and it was something I looked forward to. I lived for the weekend when I was working in the corporate world and saw nothing wrong with this. Everyone was doing it. Plus, I was functional, showing up, achieving my goals and making bank so why would I think there was something wrong. I was popular and regarded as a social character at work, always game for a good time. The problem was that I never knew when to stop. I'd get obliterated where others would stop, I'd go on to afterparty after afterparty where others would go home.

Needless to say, the recriminations, the guilt and the shame were enough to send me into a repetitive cycle of self-destruction. I got so tired of never being able to trust what I was even thinking; was this what I really thought, or was I on a comedown, was I tired, needing a snack or all of the above. It was relentless, and also served to have me run like fuck from my own life.

On and on this went for many years, until something wildly unexpected happened that would be a wake-up call I'd never forget. The curveball that came my way was in the form of a pregnancy after a one-night stand on a cocaine-fuelled night out. My response at the time was one of massive shock and denial. This wasn't happening. I couldn't be a mother, are you crazy?! I could barely look after myself! At that time, I was 36 years old, a holiday rep back in the UK between summer seasons abroad. I was due to fly back out to Spain that April for a promotion to team leader and another summer of fun in the sun. And now this?! Noooooooooo. This didn't fit my plan.

3 days later however, I was suddenly hit with the epiphany that this child had been sent to me to save my life. I truly believe that, and I will always, ALWAYS be grateful for this pivotal moment. In a moment of clarity, I recognised that this was a chance for redemption, the opportunity to turn my life around and make something of myself. It gave me a reason to be, a purpose, something to channel my love into and focus on. Something that meant I wasn't just left with me – ugh, that thought was intolerable, I hated me, although I did not know this at the time.

At this point, my party-girl ways knew no bounds. I'd be out for 3 days at a time – sniffing, boozing and smoking cigarettes. No food, no sleep, no personal hygiene. It was a pure party, and I loved it…For those 3 days. The next 3 days would be horrendous. The comedown, the bone-weariness, the moods, the emotional mess, the recriminations, the self-hate, the negative inner voice, the feeling of having fucked up, messed up, let people down. All of it would come crashing down and bury me alive beneath it. I couldn't cope with those feelings. So, I'd do it again, using cocaine to solve problems that cocaine had caused! This upside-down logic is the logic of an addict, through and through. It made perfect sense at the time. Duh, OF COURSE this was the way to fix it. Make it go away. But did it go away?! What do you think?! This just exacerbated it and around we'd go.

When I look back now, I can see that this was a very dangerous slippery slope I was on. A huge downwards spiral. I was working, somehow holding onto my job at the NHS in the interim, being paid good money, and then using that to fund my drug habit. I never had any money for luxuries or even regular things, like a meal out...I'd always have money to get supplies, but never to do anything 'normal' by this point.

Anyways, there I was, pregnant at 36 and for the first-time a feeling of hope, excitement about the future and feeling I had something to live for. I hadn't realised previously that I didn't regard my own life as worth anything, how empty it was. This only became known to me when I conceived my son and he changed everything for me. At 5 weeks pregnant, I gave up all my vices in a heartbeat, without any difficulty or regret. No repercussions and no problems, not at that time. I had the most amazing pregnancy and really started to find myself – although I still had no idea if what I thought was really what I thought or was it the hormones this time! I saved up £2k for my baby boy to buy him all the things I wanted. I felt healthy, I was sleeping, eating, connecting with friends who didn't use drugs and rebuilding relationships. Life was good. I was never going back.

Or so I thought.

Just 3 months after my son was born, I relapsed and this time the stakes were way higher. Initially it was great because I thought I was one of those people that I'd always wanted to be...the ones that can take it or leave it...I never understood those people – how could you NOT want to get totally obliterated once you started? How could you NOT be bothered about no-one answering the phone when you're trying to call it on?! All a mystery to me. So, that lasted a couple of months, where I'd just do it every 3-4 weeks and not in huge quantities – I'd sleep (eventually!) and maintain a degree of normality, I had to, I had a small baby to take care of.

Not long after this foray back into the world of addiction that I knew so well, my old tendencies resurfaced. The constant cycle of want, need, crave. The moods when I couldn't work out a way to get it into my day, the constant chasing of money to make it happen and the subsequent debts that I was never on top of because I'd pay it off then owe more at the same time. This was the time that a global pandemic suddenly shut the world down too and so I was thrown into a spin. However, this actually suited me because now I could hide and sniff as much as I wanted. I didn't tell my friends about the extent of my use because I was embarrassed, I didn't want to worry them, and I didn't want them to try and stop me. So lockdown was the perfect storm for me to snaffle away as much cocaine as I wanted without anyone really knowing. And so, I did.

It was this part of my journey that finally tipped me over the edge. I'd be waiting until my toddler went to bed to get on it so this meant I wouldn't start until 7pm. Anyone that's ever done cocaine knows that means one thing...being up all night. I'd maybe drop off around 3 or 4am and then my son would come into my room anytime from 5am. This was completely unsustainable, and it soon started to take its toll. Because I was so wiped out, the only way I could cope would be to get more, believing that this would make me a better mum because I'd be more patient with him, I'd be willing to play, I'd be more energetic. By the third or fourth day in this repeating cycle, I'd be hating myself SO MUCH, telling myself I was the worst mother, I didn't deserve to have a child, I was sick, there was something wrong with me, all of the things. So now, I don't even WANT the drugs, but I'm so fucked from days and days with very little sleep and poor eating habits, that the only way to survive is to do it more. You see where I'm going with this.

Getting off the ride wasn't an option that seemed viable or even desirable to me. This was the life I knew, and it was the one that I believed I had chosen. It was the life I always thought I'd live.

One day, I literally had enough. It packed me up more so than me packing it up. I was so done. And I quit, just like that. Since then, I have become a trained and qualified Recovery Coach, enabling me to use this lived experience and all the chaos and carnage of my previous life, to translate into something meaningful and impactful. I now help others to get off the ride, to find meaning and purpose in their own lives and to stay on track.

Of course, there's way more to this story which I shared at the start of my recovery journey on Facebook for the world to bear witness to, but for the purposes of this chapter, I want to leave you with some of my key learnings through this journey from addiction to empowerment.

Things I wish I had known sooner:

I am not my addiction. It is separate from me and does not define me.

Hiding how much I was doing was a red flag, I needed help way before I got it.

Recovery is possible – I had no idea what quitting drugs might look like, who I'd be without cocaine or how I'd be without it. What I've found is that I figure it out as I go and it's way easier and more liberating than I expected.

Feelings are going to start to make themselves known. I was going to have to deal with them in a new way and be OK with that.

Our stories have power and sharing my story was going to inspire, motivate and help many, many others. Every time I share, I heal a bit more too.

I needed healing – I was running from myself and my emotions for over two decades.

That I had a choice to change, that I even could change.

The drugs didn't make me more interesting, funny or popular...turns out that's actually who I am.

The value of connection – I felt very isolated in my addiction and it felt like there was no one who could truly understand me. This was completely untrue as I've discovered through connecting with the recovery community and other peer groups where I thrive.

I had to have these experiences in order to bring me to the place where I am now – a qualified Recovery Coach helping others who want to transform their lives.

Acts of service are an anchor – helping others in even the smallest of ways has a buzz like no other.

The consequences – real or imagined – of confessing what I was up against were way less damaging to me than living a double life, a life that was a lie. Even if the worst thing I could imagine came to pass, I knew that if I were standing on a foundation of truth, that I would get through whatever came my way.

These Are The 8 Actions That Transformed My Life:

- Admit it – First to yourself (that's the biggest one in my opinion), and then to someone you trust.
- Seek help – There are many different pathways to recovery and no one-size-fits-all solution. Examples are, finding a recovery coach, fellowships, online

support groups, hypnotherapy and more.

- Commit to this path – Make a list of pain. This is a list detailing all your transgressions, all the things that your addiction has cost you from your word being worth nothing, to the lies told, the people let down, all of it. This is an unpleasant task at best but it serves its purpose because when addiction comes for you (and it will) – you can go to this list of truths and stay on the straight and narrow. Addiction will try and tell you that it's a good idea and is very seductive and crafty in its approach. This list of pain will give you the reality of what'll happen if you believe the lies of addiction.
- Be kind to yourself – Feelings will come up that have been suppressed for a long time, you will need to learn to navigate these with self-compassion and patience. Healing takes time and relationships may take some time to rebuild too. Keep going.
- Seek out others that understand you – I fully endorse connecting with others in recovery whether that be through an organised fellowship or community, or following people in recovery on social media, going to events etc. I always advocate finding a mentor too, someone that will cheer you on and walk with you on this journey.
- Be willing to look inside yourself – What are your triggers? What needs addressing, releasing or healing?
- Be honest – This is a biggie though because we've likely spent a lot of time lying (to ourselves at minimum) so it's kind of ingrained. Time to unlearn this.
- Have a plan for bad days – Who can you call? What can you distract yourself with? What do you need in order to maintain your commitment?

I will leave you with this thought: When will you make the decision that you know will transform your own life so dramatically?

***

Sarah is a dedicated Recovery Coach Professional, who shares her transformative journey in this captivating book collaboration. With authenticity as her compass, she guides individuals toward their own path of recovery. Sarah's triumphant story over addiction showcases what is possible, creating safety for others to share their own struggles. In her chapter, " From Addiction To Empowerment," she embodies her mission—inspiring change and guiding others to a life of freedom and purpose. Through her words, Sarah unlocks readers' potential for transformation, establishing herself as an indispensable voice in this inspiring collection. You can find me @sarahrecoverycoach

Who's That Girl

Naomi Shepherd

There she was – a girl full of joy, fun, and an insatiable curiosity.
"Who's that girl?" I would wonder whilst my carefree spirit
was embracing me. But life was about to take an unexpected
turn, leading me into the grips of an abusive relationship that
dimmed my high spirits. This chapter tells the story of that
girl – her struggles, the dark moments she endured, and the
strength that pulled her through. A journey of breaking free
from fear and rediscovering the girl I thought was lost forever.

I was the 19-year-old girl living in the YMCA in my own
little flat due to being homeless the year before because of the
pressures of living at home. I was working full-time, driving
my own car, and even had a lovely boyfriend after a few bad
ones who were popular, but players and I always ended up
getting hurt. But he was different, he was my cousin's best
friend, he was 23 but wasn't my normal type. He was caring,
gentle, supportive, and really into me, he wasn't the best-
looking lad, and I didn't really fancy him, it was because I just
felt safe with him as my cousin would always say what a nice
lad he was. He used to do things like iron my work uniform

and cook my dinner after my shifts. I should have been happy and lucky to have found a man that put me first and wanted to look after me, but no, 19-year-old me was put off by this as it made me feel he wanted to settle down and things were moving too quickly.

A few weeks later he took me away up north to meet his parents as this was where he grew up. I met his friends and family, and I really did get on with them. Still, something didn't feel right, I was bored, and sex wasn't the greatest either. I tried to stay with him as I knew he would be gutted if I ended things and my cousin would have been disappointed too. 2 months into our relationship someone else caught my eye whilst I was at work. This man was working as a labourer opposite my work. They would all come in for their lunch a few times a week. He made it clear he fancied me, but his English was not the best as he was Greek (or so I thought!). He kept asking to take me out on a date, I kept telling him I was with someone, but he just kept asking every time he came in and we got chatting one day on my lunch break.

There was just something about the fact he was foreign and seemed the romantic type too and I fancied him. One evening me and my work friend went back to his flat with his friend who fancied my friend. So, it was just the 4 of us and I really didn't think anything would happen. I didn't want to cheat on my boyfriend, but I just wanted some fun. I missed the feeling of being wooed by a man and I suppose I wanted to know I still had options. Alcohol was involved and one thing led to another. I didn't sleep with this man but was so close to it, but my conscience kicked in. I did see this man a few times after, we kissed and did other stuff, but I still didn't want to sleep with him until I had finished with my boyfriend.

A holiday was booked to the Isle of Wight for me, my boyfriend, my cousin, and my best friend. One whole week with a man I really wasn't into anymore and who was also falling in love with me which made it even harder for me to finish things. During the holiday my boyfriend started talking about our future together and planning to get a flat together and maybe even moving up north near his family. I really had to finish things, so 3 months into my relationship with a man who adored me and wanted to give me a good life, I ended things. He was devastated. He broke down in my flat. At first, he just cried and tried to hug me, asking if there was something wrong with him. Was he too nice? Should he be less caring? Would I prefer him to be like my past boyfriends? I hated myself for treating him like that, but he just wasn't the one for me and I still believe today that I did the right thing back then. I lost a lot of friends due to the fact I started a relationship with a man who clearly went on to not be the person I thought, and the excitement disappeared just as quickly as it arrived.

Two months later I ended up moving into a flat share with some friends. I was earning good money, working full time, paying my bills, and even having my own little kitten. Life was good, but things started to change when I found out this man that I was seeing was Albanian and not Greek. It didn't bother me, but the lies bothered me. Lies were one of his specialities, he even lied about his age, lied about where he was, lied about money, lied about what jobs he was doing, I just put it to the back of my mind as I really was certain he wouldn't cheat on me as he didn't need to, sex was great and even on times I didn't feel like it I still obliged to keep him happy. I stopped going clubbing because he didn't like me going out without him. I stopped a lot of things that I enjoyed doing just to please him. I was adamant I could change him, and I ignored all the red flags that everyone around me could see.

On my 20th birthday, we went clubbing with friends and I was so up for it, but my boyfriend wasn't. He gave in and came with us, the night ended badly as he got in a fight with some bloke and he got thrown out, so we all had to come home. He was very drunk, and we argued outside my flat and it ended with me getting slapped around the face. I should have realised at this point that this man was not who I thought he was at the start, he wasn't the romantic guy I assumed he was, he wasn't the man who was going to look after me or respect me. But I somehow was convinced we should stay together, and I could change him. After all, every time he hit me he was so sorry and would treat me so nicely for a few days after so it was in him to be different. 4 months into the relationship I fell pregnant, he was very aware I wasn't on the pill, and he chose not to use protection. I deep down wanted a baby, again for some reason I thought having his baby would change him. How wrong was I? He did ask me to get an abortion, but I made it clear there was no way I was going to do that. I said I would have the baby with or without him and knew he would come around to the idea. I soon got talked into moving in with him at his flatshare where other Albanian men lived so that I could save more money for the baby, but we would get our own place before the baby was born.

So here I was pregnant, still working full time, living basically in one room as I was told I couldn't spend time in the main lounge where the other men were. He would go mad if I came out. They spent most nights drinking vodka and playing cards for money. They would speak in their language so I had no idea what they would be talking about. It soon became apparent he had a gambling addiction and I found myself often bailing him out due to him losing his money in fruit machines or playing cards. Things got so bad one day, he pinned me against the wall of a fruit machine establishment in town forcing me to give him more money. The security pulled him off me and I just ran home but ended up in hospital with high blood pressure for a few days. Did I end things with him? No, all I kept thinking was he apologises and doesn't mean it and I want my baby to have its dad around. I don't want to do this on my own.

Two months before my baby was born, I moved into my own flat, but he didn't want to be on the tenancy, so I paid for everything by myself. He would stay most nights and give me money towards some bills but only then to take it back off me for drink or cigarettes. One evening I won £1000 at bingo, I had plans to spend it on the baby but straight away he said he needed to send his family some money in Albania so I ended up with half of it. All these little things that were happening to me didn't seem a big deal at the time I suppose, because all I wanted was for us to be a family once the baby was born and kept thinking he would see the baby and change instantly.

We had lots of bad arguments during my pregnancy, and I was in the hospital about 4 times with my blood pressure and other complications but ended up being 7 days overdue when I went into labour and he was nowhere to be seen. My mum picked me up that evening and took me to the hospital. We had messaged him but didn't get a reply for hours. Eventually, he turned up at the hospital and had been drinking. He fell asleep on the floor for most of the labour and woke up just before our baby girl was born. Just as I thought, he seemed smitten with her, I could see the love in his eyes and he had a tear when he held her. Things were ok for a few weeks after. He helped quite a bit but his controlling ways were getting worse. I wasn't allowed to breastfeed if any other men were around. I would get told to go to another room. He still disappeared for days and went out at night after work and did not come home till the next day. When the baby was 3 months, we moved to another little house I had found and again he wouldn't go on the tenancy so I had to claim benefits as a single parent until I went back to work. He still stayed at the house some nights when he wasn't at work which he did night shifts, or so he told me anyway. The arguments got worse as he made me so insecure, he was mentally abusive as well as physically and I even felt forced to sleep with him when I didn't want to, but I never saw it as that bad because he was my partner, and he didn't pin me down. I just used to give in because I knew there would be physical arguments otherwise.

I was losing weight dramatically. People would mention it to me but I brushed it off even though I weighed 6 stone at one point and could see my bones sticking out. I was so depressed I didn't even realise I wasn't eating properly and I wasn't sleeping much as my baby didn't sleep much. I most probably had postnatal depression, but I hid it well from everyone. The arguments carried on, I would run up my road after him when he used to walk out begging him not to leave, I would take my daughter out in the car just to go looking for him, I was so desperate to be a proper family and not end up being another single young mum that I ignored all the bad things that were affecting my daughter because I thought it was better for her to have both parents instead of just a happy mum. The neighbours started to get concerned as well and called the police a few times due to all the shouting. I was oblivious to the fact this wasn't good for any of us, I had grown up with my parents arguing badly so I assumed it was part of being in a relationship. It actually took me almost 4 years of this toxic relationship to realise I had lost myself; I wasn't me; I was drained with so much upset and abuse and fear for both me and my now 2-year-old daughter that I knew something had to change. I couldn't stay with a man like that just so my daughter had her dad around because it could end up so badly.

I asked myself who would want me? a single 23-year-old with a 2-year-old, I wasn't the girl full of joy and curiosity, or the girl with the carefree spirit and the world at her feet to do what she wanted, instead I had lost all that to one person who I thought was my world but he tore it apart. But he gave me one thing that meant I could fix it back together again; my little girl and she was truly my world. So, after another physical argument on my 23rd birthday, I knew I had to end it. I was scared to tell him and knew he would hardly see his daughter once he left and I was right he disappeared from her life 1 year after I ended things and said he knew he wasn't good enough to be her dad, this was something I had dreaded but it made me more determined to be both mum and dad to her and give her all the love she needed. I did meet someone else who I went on to marry and have 2 more children with and for 18 years I had my little family.

As I end this chapter, I can't help but remember "Who's that girl" – the happy, curious, and fun-loving version of myself. Life's challenges and an abusive relationship dimmed my high spirits for a while. But through this journey of self-discovery, I've found her again. It hasn't been easy, but it's shown me that we all have the power to rediscover ourselves and be who we truly want to be, finding ourselves is possible, I did this by knowing I was doing the best I could to be a mum, doing things I enjoyed doing, training to be a therapist and helping people to feel better.

So let this chapter inspire you as it has me, finding ourselves is possible and worth every step to shine brighter than ever before.

***

I'm Naomi, the author of the chapter "who's that girl". A mum to a teenage son and 2 adult daughters. I'm also a cat and dog mum too, they are treated like they are my children sometimes.

I have been a holistic therapist for 8 years. I feel that massage as well as reflexology can not only help us to feel physically well but mentally too as our everyday stresses build up in our bodies. I know that if we don't look after ourselves, we can lose ourselves, which I did for a while in the past but I hope that my chapter can show that we need to put ourselves first sometimes to find ourselves again. I am so grateful to be able to take part in this collaboration and share times of sadness that I managed to turn into times of resilience.

https://www.facebook.com/Naomisoultouch

RISE OF THE FEMININE

Cheryl Beckworth

Change is happening.
The shift has begun.
Are you ready?
Now is your time...
The feminine is rising.

As the world awakens to the power and potential of female voices, a new era is rising: an era which embraces a more feminine way of being.

I'm Cheryl, a Manifest Mentor with my own business, Grounded Goddess, which includes a manifesting community and membership, an online shop selling powerful healing crystals, a podcast, and a journal.

Manifesting, moon magic, and crystals are my passions, but lifting and supporting women, in every aspect of their lives, is my true mission.

As a director of a wellbeing community centre, co-leader of a women's group, and creator of an online community, I've seen the pattern all too often: women putting the needs of their partner or children or community or job before their own aspirations and needs.

Not only do they put their own wants and needs at the bottom of the list, they often lose sight of what it is they really want.

To rebuild this connection, I introduce women to the world of manifesting and affirmations, giving them the permission and the tools needed to prioritise themselves, practise self-care, set big goals for their own lives, and most importantly to understand that they are not alone because the Universe has their back and is ready to guide them on their way.

As I sat down to write this chapter, with all the ideas I wanted to share with you swirling round in my head, my own feminine intuition spoke up. I knew I had to call out this disconnection that women have with their own voice, their own intuition, and help them to see their own connection to the Universe.

I'll share my personal journey to embrace who I am, celebrate all my magic feminine energies, listen to my inner knowing, and lean into my body and its needs.

DISCONNECTION WITH THE FEMININE

Women putting themselves first and striving for their own goals is sadly lacking in our society. With a historic expectation that women put others first, and now juggle family responsibilities with careers, they can feel pulled in a million directions but not sure where they are heading.

I was no different to this and for many years I was completely disconnected from my own feminine energy.

Throughout my teens and early 20s, I always felt like a tomboy, one of the lads. I never had any real close female friends. If I'm honest I thought they were all catty, bitchy and fake. This meant I wasn't surrounded by other women celebrating their feminine voices or being encouraged to speak up using my own.

In this very patriarchal society, success looks like being driven, setting high targets, being busy, and working 24/7. And, for a long time, I thought the same. I felt the pressure to hustle so I could be successful in my career or life, to work that little bit harder, to push myself to the limits of exhaustion. I always started work early, finished late, and worked through lunch.

As a result, like clockwork, I would burn out every three months.

I never trusted my gut feeling, that deep knowing that tells you something isn't quite right. I ignored my inner voice to my own detriment.

It wasn't until I reconnected with my feminine energy and allowed it to rise within me that my life completely changed. Embracing your own feminine energy is an essential part of ensuring you are happy, aligned, in balance, and successful.

One part of your feminine voice you should listen to is your inner cycle. After all, what is more feminine than menstruation?

THE MOST POWERFUL CYCLE

Growing up, I hated my period with a passion. To be fair, it only used to visit twice a year but when it did it absolutely crippled me. I could barely move for 3 days, snuggled up with a hot water bottle, under a duvet, hating my body, and hating being a woman. I honestly believed my period was against me and I'd never be able to conceive, or at best really struggle and need medical interventions.

But when you understand your menstrual cycle, it's a powerful way to understand and nurture yourself.

We are creatures of a cyclic nature. Cycles surround us: day and night, the seasons, the moon, life and death. And, as women, we all have our very own inner cycles. How often do you listen and follow yours? This is the cycle that will impact us the greatest. Why then don't we pay more attention to our own inner cycles?

For most of the women I speak to, the full influence of their cycle is still a complete mystery. It's the cycle that causes them the most issues too. PMT, painful cramping, anxiety, heavy bleeding, completely irregular patterns, or non-existent periods.

As women, it's expected that we provide for, love and nurture everyone ALL the time. But we aren't built this way. Our cycles are a clear indication that we need time to recover, rest and restore our body, mind, and soul. If only we would pay attention.

YOUR FOUR SEASONS

If you want a life that is aligned with the flow of your own energy, I encourage you to be aware of your internal cycle. And by this, I don't just mean when your period starts and stops. Understanding my full four week cycle not only changed my life – regular monthly, pain-free periods and three beautiful babies, but I have seen this transformation in so many other women too.

So, your monthly cycle is broken down into four weeks, each with a corresponding 'season'.

Week 1 – Winter

This is what I call bleed week. It is a time when you need to retreat inwards, semi-hibernate, and practise lots of self-care. It is a time for less plans, less work, less action.

Your body needs to be nourished with good food and your essence needs to experience self-care. I have a 'Moon

Box' full of all my necessities for upping my self-care game. It includes items such as beautiful bath oil, candles, my moon cup, crystals for healing and self-love, and, most importantly – chocolate!

Winter is when we are most in tune with our inner knowing. This is a time for listening and connecting with your intuition. Make notes of what ideas arise for you, ready to implement in spring.

Week 2 – Spring

Yay! We are moving into spring and welcoming back the light. Take full advantage of this increase in energy.

This is a time when you tend to be full of new ideas. You are blossoming. You feel fabulous. Your energy is reigniting.

Start making plans and setting the path for growing ideas from Winter or Spring into reality.

You may feel ready to take action, especially towards the end of the week.

Week 3 – Summer

We all love summer, right? This is when you will be buzzing with energy and loving life. You will be most productive and confident during Summer.

All the self-doubt and criticism you had earlier in your cycle has gone; our inner critic is taking a much needed rest. You'll feel ready to take action: host those meetings, meet with clients, socialise with friends, really get moving.

Plan for any big projects, like a garage clear out or launching something new in your business for this week.

Week 4 – Autumn

Autumn is when you start to slow down. This is a time when you can be very self-critical. You may question your abilities and feel not good enough. But remember that it is just your hormones tricking you. Your inner critic is being an absolute bitch. Once you know this and acknowledge that it is just her and your hormones talking, it's easier for you to put her back in a box and ignore those thoughts too!

During my Autumn, I often question what I'm doing, if I can actually achieve what I want. I say things like 'Who did I think I was? I can never…' But just knowing it's my hormones talking allows me to just let it go and stop being so harsh to myself.

This is a week where you may resist showing up. Don't make challenging appointments for this week. Be gentle with yourself and listen to your energy needs.

When you are aware of your full cycle, you can work with your energy each week. By adapting your life and business, you can make the most of your natural flow.

There have even been scientific studies showing that, when women work 3-week months and take time off to recoup during their bleed week, they are much more productive than when they work a full month.

Spain has even recently introduced paid leave for women with painful periods, acknowledging the impact our cycles have on our productivity and energy. How amazing is this advancement in understanding women's cycles?

I encourage you all to take time to track your inner cycle and understand your own energies and needs. It's a real game changer. I'll often notice when I'm working too hard, and not in flow, my periods are so much more painful, now I understand it's my body's way of telling me to slow down and refill my cup.

MORE WAYS TO CONNECT TO YOUR FEMININE VOICE

As well as connecting with your cycle, there are many other ways to connect with the feminine voice you have ready to roar inside you.

- Listen to your intuition

Listening to your intuition will help you to make better decisions and connect with others on a deeper level. Quiet time is key for this. In our busy world, we need to make an effort to escape outside noise and listen to our inner voice. Make time to meditate and ask to receive guidance and knowledge about your journey.

- Write in a journal

Journaling is a way to release your thoughts and emotions, explore your deepest feelings, and reflect on your life. Making time to jot down your thoughts is incredibly beneficial for processing all the information you absorb each day. Grab a pen and paper and simply write down your thoughts, feelings, and experiences. You may be surprised to see ideas solidify or become clearer when you just allow yourself to keep writing.

- Use empathy

Empathy is a key aspect of feminine energy which helps you connect with others more deeply. Take time to really listen and gain a deeper understanding of their perspective, then use this to help guide your actions. Be sure to retain the balance between caring for your own needs and the needs of others.

- Be open

Being vulnerable is often seen as a weakness and there is an expectation that you shouldn't show your struggles or cry, that these types of feelings should be hidden behind closed doors. But vulnerability can be a strength. By being open and authentic, you create more trust with those around you. It's okay not to be perfect and happy all the time. It's ok to be upset, angry, frustrated. Your feminine voice doesn't have to be sunshine and rainbows all the time.

The times in my business where I've been vulnerable have honestly been the most powerful in helping others. When I've opened up about difficulties, I get so many messages from other women that the circumstances have resonated with them. They feel better that they are not alone in their situation and realise that there isn't anything wrong with them, and this makes everything seem easier to cope with and more manageable.

• Call in your tribe

Allow yourself to be held and supported. This will change your life. We aren't meant to live alone and in isolation. We can use our feminine power to lift each other up, to get the support we need, and to make our own voices stronger and more powerful.

Try to find a group or membership where 'your tribe' is at. In my many years of holding space for women, the changes I've seen in women's lives from finding their tribe, being heard and feeling supported brings me to tears. I've witnessed the confidence of so many women grow: from being agoraphobic to getting a full time job, from feeling they can't do anything in life to starting their own business, from doubting their self worth to publishing their very own book! Just knowing that someone is in your corner cheering you on, that someone has your back, can help you to accomplish incredible things.

It's Time To Rise

Right here, right now, I am giving you permission to listen to your inner voice, to connect with and respect the feminine energy of your cycle, and to ask for exactly what you need!

As a woman, you have a powerful voice that deserves to be heard. Listen to your voice and share it. The Universe wants to hear you.

***

Cheryl Beckworth is a Manifest Mentor, White Witch and Author. Manifesting, Moon Magic and Crystals are Cheryl's passions. Lifting and supporting women, in every aspect of their lives, is her mission. Cheryl talks a lot about manifesting but her success wasn't from just 'asking the universe' and it suddenly happened overnight. Cheryl also took inspired consistent action. With this in mind, she mentors women via her M.A.G.I.C™ system to empower them to reach their goals and desires! Cheryl looks at both sides of your life, personal and business. Both need to work in perfect synchronicity in order to create success and happiness. Cheryl also runs Grounded Goddess, her business selling beautiful and powerful healing crystals. 'Together, we can start you on the path to getting aligned with your business and your needs, creating that balance, so you can live the life you want'. You will find Cheryl mainly hanging out on Facebook @ groundedgoddessx or at www.cherylbeckworth.com

A Goddess Can Be Destroyed (But Only For One More Day)

Nixie Foster

I was too scared to go to the toilet without asking, a fully grown woman and I would have preferred to wet myself than go without asking. Two things came from this. At the time, I thanked the goddess for my discovery of panty liners and secondly over a decade later the shock and tears when I found myself writing that sentence. You see as my sister put it, I was a fierce, beautiful, and slightly terrifying lion goddess of a teenager and young woman. I was an activist for animal rights, women's rights, and Amnesty International, heck I even broke a nearly six-foot-tall fifth former's (that's year 11 at school) nose for picking on one of my fellow second formers (year 8) who now would be recognised as neurodivergent but back then, way back then, in the eighties was given an unkind label. I ran bars and pubs and would chuck 22-stone bikers out if they didn't behave. I was strong, confident, and took no shit. Until I did.

I cannot pinpoint the day it changed or why. I know a few months earlier I had had my heart broken, the whole heart ripped out of my chest feeling of pain and numbness. I know I was walking around in a fog. I still to this day do not know how I was swept up into the relationship that was to last over a decade and spiral me into the darkness of domestic violence. This story isn't about all those details or the nitty gritty, they are not my focus today. My focus is the moment I shattered into a million pieces and when I came back together, none of those pieces were in the same place and some were missing forever.

Many of you will think this is the day I escaped, the day I said no more, the day my abuser left my life – but it wasn't. That day was a good few years before the moment that I shattered, the moment I became a mother to my youngest son. The moment when my world changed, when I realised that my worth was thought of as less because I was a mother. This is the moment when my anchor, the moon, truly stepped up and I reclaimed slowly the lioness goddess and her beautiful fierceness, a work still in progress. So let me introduce my old friend and anchor in my life, the moon. It is the world's oldest temple and is closely linked to the divine feminine energies, intuition, instincts, and represents female empowerment. And boy did I need that with the chaotic and overwhelming life of a new mum. My dreams of how it was meant to be had been shattered and scattered into a million pieces but the moon showed me it didn't have to be this way. I am going to show you how moon alignment can bring back clarity and purpose, and help you find direction back to your true self.

I had desperately wanted to be the woman I had dreamed to be, which had been stolen from me first through a teenage pregnancy with a birth trauma and then domestic violence of the worst kind of emotional, financial, sexual, and mental abuse. He had tried the threat of physical violence but the lioness wouldn't take that, she would protect herself and fight back, so the full destruction of my sense of self began. The moon always shone after hiding in the dark and her beauty brought a little joy every time. Memories of a child watching the moon with my dad and the anchor of wonder she had placed in my heart when I was a small child. So, it made sense I returned to her to heal.

Our feminine cycles are interlinked with the phases of the moon and its cycles. Just like the moon begins her cycle at the new moon and then waxes to the full moon and wanes back to the new moon so too do we as a woman.

The new moon represents the menstrual part of our cycle followed by waxing to ovulation at the full moon and waning back to release. In ancient times the moon coincided with each woman's cycle but in modern times we follow different calendars and have artificial light. We're not sleeping at the rising of the moon and waking up at the rising of the sun. When I started attuning and aligning with the moon and my cycles my body followed and I felt much more naturally aligned with my energies and much less fighting against the ebbs and flows of feminine energy.

THE TRIPLE GODDESS

Just as the moon reflects our monthly cycles so too does she reflect our life as cyclical beings. We ebb and flow in our life stages and our daily emotions. In a society and world that doesn't support us as a woman, mother, and badass goddess we easily become overwhelmed, undervalued, and burnout trying to be and live how we dreamed it to be. That is where moon alignment begins to bring harmony into your life.

Let's take a look at that simplified:

- Maiden – The Waxing Moon – Your Carefree Youth, The New Beginning or A Beginning
- Mother – The Full Moon – The Moment When It All Comes Together
- Crone – The Waning Moon – The Knowledge or Lesson Learnt

There are many other phases throughout your life such as woman and wise woman. There are eight phases of the moon and each is linked to particular energies and actions. It is through aligning with the moon's energies that you can recognise these in your everyday life. When you do the transformation truly begins – living in alignment with your rhythms, creating a map to embracing your cyclical self, and striking balance with the universe's rhythms, twists, and turns. It was in these moments I truly began to heal. It was in the arms of the moon's energy that I unlocked my voice and began my journey to helping women become empowered and share their voices too. I began sharing my work with the moon, connecting with women on a similar path, and others who felt called to myself and awakening their feminine energies.

The Eight Phases Of The Moon

So, what are the eight phases and their energies?

- New – set goals and intentions, a time for new beginnings, rejuvenation, and dreams.
- Waxing Crescent – having faith and courage in your dreams, take steps to move forward.

- First Quarter – meet obstacles and challenges head-on, to heal emotionally and spiritually.
- Waxing Gibbous – put actions on hold, tweak, and adjust to prepare for the full moon.
- Full – release intentions and goals that aren't serving you, forgive, and be grateful.
- Waning Gibbous – relax, accept, and regroup, transmute low vibe and negative energies into positive ones.
- Last Quarter – re-evaluate and trust, declutter, and remove attachments not serving you.
- Waning Crescent – heal and soothe self, surrender, meditate, and plan for the new moon.

It seems a little overwhelming to begin with but aren't you totally overwhelmed already and juggling what feels like a billion and one things? Aren't you already sacrificing YOU and giving your all to everyone else? How would you feel if you could step out from those shadows and into the light of feeling in control and being true to yourself? Let's delve a little deeper into how moon alignment can bring you clarity and purpose; empowering you to discover your true self.

Let's start at the beginning of the moon's 29 ½ day cycle – the new moon. It's a new lunar month and a chance to decide on the one thing that you want to achieve for that time, just one thing. It could be something simple like having a pamper bath once a week undisturbed or something big like starting your own business. It is totally up to you.

You will need to know the phase that the moon is in so hop online and print out a moon phase calendar for your specific time zone.

As the moon moves into the waxing crescent you will begin to hear that mind monkey whispering things like who do you think you are, you don't deserve this, give up now before you are disappointed. Keep faith, find ways to stay focused, and shut up the mind monkey. Don't go overloading yourself with a new meditation routine that takes hours that won't work for you. Maybe it's a walking meditation in the woods with or without your family or brewing yourself a mindful cuppa.

The first quarter is going to hit you with obstacles and challenges but face them. Trust in the energy of Mother Moon, she is calling out your divine feminine. Acknowledge that you have some healing to do on an emotional and spiritual level. The word to focus on is healing, not healed. Remember small aligned steps and you have 13 moon cycles to take you through the year; each with a new moon and full moon that focuses on different areas, energies, and aspects of your life.

Next comes the waxing gibbous and it is time to pause, halt, stop, cease – you get the idea – any actions that you are taking in working towards your goal and dream set at the new moon. Take a look at what inspired actions you have been taking to achieve your intentions. Does anything need tweaking? Is something not working? Are you struggling with or fighting against the steps and actions you are taking? Have these clear in your mind ready for the full moon.

In comes the full moon with her energy. The time when she seems to have the greatest pull on you as a soul-centred spiritual woman. Now is the time to perform your forgiveness and gratitude ritual. Now is the time to release any actions, intentions, or goals that aren't actually serving you WITHOUT GUILT. Let's face it, we are just adding to the overwhelm or crappy feelings if we keep trying to do, feel, create, or be something that isn't aligned with our truth. And sometimes we don't actually know what that truth is until we begin to gain clarity and purpose through connecting to our divine feminine energies, moon work or alignment certainly brings out that goddess aspect.

After the intensity of the moon's energy when she is full, she brings us the waning gibbous, phew! Take a breath, relax, and regroup. Get this low vibe energy that drains the get-up and go out of us into high vibe sing and dance (if you want) energy that lights us up and get back to taking inspired action that is totally aligned with your new adjusted intention.

The last quarter is when you can feel a little bit OMG I haven't achieved what I set out to do and the end of the moon cycle is nearly here. Let me tell you it's ok. Spend this phase decluttering your home, workspace, phone, emails, or your own self. Take out and remove any stuff, blocks that are keeping you disconnected from your true self or achieving your goal.

As the waning crescent leads you back into the new moon and new beginnings, surrender your goals and trust that you have done what was in alignment with your energies and guided by the moon's energies. Heal, soothe, and get ready for the next new moon. Remember it doesn't have to be perfect, and it doesn't have to be fully manifested, especially if it's a big goal or dream, then take stock to see what achievements and progress you have made, not just on your intentions but also on yourself and the journey to being empowered to be who you want to be.

And so, let's cycle back to my story. I could tell you of the horrors and humiliation of being a victim of domestic violence, but I have told that part of my story before. I could tell you about the moments I walked away and the rose quartz that saved my life because if I had stayed just one more day, I truly believe I would not have come out of the relationship alive. I could tell you about the shame that even now I sometimes feel. I could tell you about the isolation, the destruction of relationships with family and friends. But I won't because I have previously, and this book is about 'Hear Me Evolve' and everyone's on their own evolving journey, everyone is at a different stage, following a different path, and has different experiences. Mine is now about my voice and the power becoming a mother brought me. It awakened the fierceness within, and I began to live the life I wanted. I still have a whole heap of evolving awaiting me and each day I strive to achieve one more small turn of the wheel with the help of Mother Moon. But for now, my Little Moon is the shining light to remind me that I deserve to be loved, I am loved, and I can be the goddess lion changing the world for women to be heard and create a better future for my son.

***

Nixie is a Storyteller, Illustrator, Author and Founder of Holistic Storytelling Publishing House and the movement S.H.E. Aloud. She heals the whole and empowers women by unlocking their voices through books, writing, workshops, journalling, podcasts, talks, and more.

Her mission is to create inclusive communities bringing women and feminine beings together and reignite the power of storytelling. Her vision is to help women unlock their voices to create empowerment, archives, and immersive experiences accessible to all creating a world that is better and does better for women.

www.nixiefoster.com

OFF THE ROLLERCOASTER INTO MY LOWER TOX LANE

Aisling Louise Owens Nash

Before I began the journey I am now on, which is one of health, lower tox habits, and creating a life I love, my days looked extremely different from what they are now. I would spend my nights tossing and turning and switching on the bedroom lamps to read so I could fall back asleep. I would wake, try to stand and I would feel a whoosh and then I would run those 4 or 5 steps to my bathroom sink to heave. I would get myself going once the heaving passed and I had expelled all that could be expelled from my tummy.

I would go down the stairs and make a Nespresso, prepare my son's lunch for school, and exhaustedly dress him, feed him, wrap up his brother and sister, make another Nespresso, down it in one, then get everyone in the car to drive to school drop-offs. I would get home and have another Nespresso or I would go out for breakfast with other mammies and drink tea with milk and lots of sugar. I was perpetually stressed, either on a high of energy and doing all the things or struggling to be motivated to do anything. I 'got through' the days. That's it. A day on repeat – like the loop de loop on this rollercoaster of life, exhaustion, hormones, stress, mood swings, and feeling sick all the time.

My eldest child was finally at the point of receiving some further support and assessments for his needs. My 2nd child started Montessori and there were some issues but I didn't make much of them as he could eat with cutlery, he was a great little chatterbox and he could help get himself dressed. The total opposite of his older dyspraxic brother. My daughter was quite young but had been experiencing illness and multiple hospital stays within a few months. So, life was stressful, emotional, and exhausting. I was also filling out pages of paperwork for a support payment for parents with children whose needs are far in excess of their peers. I had never known it existed and I also hadn't realised that the care I was providing was not normal. As soon as this was authorised, I applied for a leave of absence from my job protecting my role for 2 years. It was a temporary leave and, in my mind, I could sort all the issues out at that time. It was never meant to be permanent. I was starting to move past all this until one day I went food shopping alone and I experienced a panic attack whilst driving. I had driven past the turning to my unsupportive GP triggering the panic attack and causing me to accidentally hit the accelerator instead of the brakes. I was frozen and couldn't move my foot off the wrong pedal. I crashed into the last vehicle at the lights and caused a ripple effect where 3 cars were damaged. Mine plus 2 others. I knew then I needed to change GPs.

I was diagnosed with PND (Post Natal Depression) &

prescribed medication. I was still breastfeeding so I read that tiny piece of paper that folds out the size of a small table back to front and realised the purpose was to boost my serotonin levels. I spoke to my new GP and said I recognised I needed the help and medication but I did not want to become reliant on it. I searched out and read papers on what can help boost your serotonin naturally – which foods and habits could help. And so followed dance parties with my kid in the kitchen and in their bedrooms, eating my 'happy foods', listening to audiobooks. A little over 3 months later I spoke with my GP and moved away from my medication. I was in more control. Was I still pretty exhausted? Yes! Was I still nauseous most mornings and headachy? Yes. Was I still cranky mammy by the evening? Unfortunately, some days I was. Was I in a better place? Was I evolving? YES!

Initially it was hard to see where to go from there, I was still feeling quite crap but I was in a better place mentally and a little better physically. I was still 'sick' most days and that was harder and harder to accept as I knew there had to be a way to be better. I had my bloods done in the women's hospital and at my bleeding disorder clinic. My daughter was hospitalised again and they told me her amino acids were low and asked if I was vegan. I was not, but it brought me on to researching again – what can I eat to help with this? I was eating high-quality meat but I realised I wasn't getting or absorbing all the nutrients. I ended up purchasing a day-of-the-week tablet box and filling it with vitamins. 9 little capsules per day were in there. It was very difficult to be consistent taking these. I have a strong gag reflex so sometimes I would end up expelling them anyway just after taking them. One day, while chatting with my cousin I mentioned this. She asked what I was taking – B vitamins,

Vitamin K, Biotin, and a few more. She said – well I drink this drink every day and it is delicious and it has all those things in it. If you are struggling with tablets and capsules why not try this?

What did I have to lose? I did it and wow, did it change my entire life! My evolution truly began. In 4 months, I had dropped 5kg of inflammation, my chronic pain from the crash was lessening, I had more energy, and focus and I even started exercising. I stopped lurking in a carers support group and started to add value and support to others and then a course on leadership came up and I decided to join it. Simultaneously I was attending a Parenting Plus course with the social work team and an OT Sensory Diet course. You see, my middle child had started school but was not even getting full hours as he had since been diagnosed with ASD and a PDA profile. If you know, you know. The journey there was so difficult and to this day I will never forget sitting with that psychologist and crying when he told me I was an amazing parent and that I was living in crisis and no, I was not a bad parent like people had been telling me. He also said we would not be put on yet another waiting list and he was creating a team especially to assess my child because he was concerned for all of our safety. That was really scary. I loved my child as he was but he was Jekyll and Hyde. As a result, the school would not let him participate fully in school so I had no time and no life. Some days I would be asked to collect him after not even 15 mins so when this course came up, I stood my ground with the school and said – they needed to suck it up and take care of him so I could learn the skills and tools I needed to better support myself and my children.

I headed off to The Philippines for my sister's wedding which I had helped plan and organise. I brought my drinks with me (they are sachets). I had at this point begun to look at what I was eating and drinking that was not helping – so yes through those drinks, I had managed to reduce my Nespresso intake which saved me a lot of money too! I returned home and 6 days later we entered the first Covid 19 lockdown. A few weeks in, my cousin asked if I would like to join her conference on Zoom, for the brand I was using the products from.

This was the next stage in my evolution – the support, the mindset work, the community, the belief systems, and the passion for protecting people and the planet just aligned so completely that I wanted to be ALL IN with this brand. I had already been sharing my love of my drinks naturally. I had also been helping some other parents at the school gate who were having challenges with their children. You see, I hadn't just made changes for myself, but the changes I did also positively impacted my children and it was being noticed in their behaviours and ability to engage. A few months later my Facebook Community was born.

Every Sunday morning myself, my cousin, and a friend of ours hosted 30 min sessions with tips for healthier living and shared some products too. It was a vehicle that supported the massive change and re-ignition of my entrepreneurial passion in me. We joined up each day over lockdown as a community at 6am for a Miracle Morning together. We worked on our mindset, and personal growth and once a week we trained together on skills to grow. It was and still is life-changing support for me. I cannot ever imagine not being part of this business, brand, and community.

I evaluated other areas of my life. How our home was set up, where we lived, and the people I was spending time with outside of this community – did they align with me? Could they come on this journey with me or would they hold me back? We decided to prepare our house and put it on the market. We went into lockdown in March 2020 and we had moved to our new home by November 2020.

I had also gone back to using essential oils and more 'natural' cleaning supplies – most of which I realise now were just greenwashed products but life and learning are a journey. Through the other brand I joined I learned about ingredients we should avoid and I regularly also utilise the website www.ewg.org to research and learn more about products, ingredients, and the environment. As we moved house, I dumped ALL the toxic cleaners and lots of clutter. This was another great catalyst for change and an opportunity to start fresh, in the countryside in a small community despite the lockdowns.

Over the last almost 4 years on this journey to lower tox living principles for life and loving life, I have totally transformed my way of thinking and how I look at life. I have become more aligned with myself and with my purpose. I am happy to say that by the end of 2020, I was no longer heaving over a sink, I was sleeping well, and I was happier, healthier, and more empowered to take back control and make those changes with conviction. Why should we just exist and go through the motions each day?? We need to take back control and find lifestyle habits that allow us to build a life we love, thrive and flourish in. We get one life, one body, one chance. It is a journey; one we should thoroughly enjoy.

My mission is to inspire others to embrace some lower-tox living swaps in their lives, simple switches, and changes, so they too can take back more control over time and build a life free of toxicity – physical, mental, and environmental.

HABITS I HAVE ADDED FOR US AS A FAMILY:

- Whole Food Cooking and Eating
- Cheats instead of Treats for the things we know are unhealthy but we still love in moderation.
- Listening to podcasts and personal development books to grow our minds and skills.
- Making and using simplified cleaning products.
- No negative news programs but still access to news in the car if it comes on.
- More music in our lives again – choosing songs that raise us up.
- Reading more – and choosing wisely what we read
- Trying new things!
- Reducing our plastic usage and carbon footprint.
- Miracle Morning practices and meditation.
- Relaxing music playing and essential oils diffusing most days in our home.
- We are slowly reducing the clutter and amount of 'stuff' in our lives.
- We ask for experiences for the children or things they actually need instead of more toys and stuff at birthdays and Christmas.

There are so many simple ways we can take back and control our lives; I now teach people how to get started and find their 'lane'. I have a roadmap, I have tried many routes, and everyone will find the lane that suits them best. I am here to guide people on a journey of exploration and education so they can choose what will fit most for themselves.

My relationships have changed with my children for the better on this journey. I now know better how to prepare for spending time with people that I do love but who drain me. I am a trustee with a charity close to my heart, I head up the work for Hopefull Handbags Global in Ireland, I look after Ireland and Northern Ireland for Mums in Business International and I run my lower tox living courses and group. I show up and deliver 20 min sessions for healthy living for free and to add value and simple actions for anyone wanting to explore more. I am starting a small business retail consultancy firm.

The thread that runs through everything I do is this – support and empowerment and education. Providing people with opportunities to connect, create community and make positive changes.

If you feel stuck right now, or resistant to change. Stop, take a deep breath, do something that brings you joy, and then sit with yourself with a piece of paper, draw a circle on it and split it in four. Grab yourself some pens/colours, don't try to think too much but draw or write words in each segment based on the following headings.

- Gifts – think about what gifts you bring to your world. What makes you, you!
- Skills/Knowledge – what skills and knowledge do you possess?
- Dreams – if there were no barriers in this life what does your dream life look like?
- Fears – what are your biggest fears?

You do not need to do all of this in one sitting, I would even suggest doing it over a period of 4-5 days. At the end, look at what you have laid out in those sections and see where you might want to embrace one thing or change one thing. Start there.

My vision for the future is to create spaces where communities can embrace holistic living and well-being practices – they can learn and grow, embracing the tools that work for them and their lifestyles. I see centres in areas of natural beauty and in towns where when you step into the space, arts, culture, health, and well-being flood you with inspiration and remind you that life is for loving and living and not just existing. It will remind people they have control; they just need to choose to take it back, embrace it and find what works for them.

Take Back Control, Make Simple Switches, Transform Your Life.

Love Life,
Aislíng x

***

Aislíng Louise Owens Nash is an Irish Mummy of 3, carer, a self confessed nerd, and she is obsessed with food! She is a female empowerment networking leader with MIB International, leading the Ireland and Northern Ireland team and the Head of Hopefull Handbags Global for Ireland. Life for Aislíng is pretty full. Her mission is to impact one individual or household per day to make positive changes for their health, the health of their family and the planet in a way that works for them using lower toxic living habits and hacks! It is all about removing toxicity in your life – physical, mental and environmental. https://www.facebook.com/AislingOwensNash or @aislingowensnash

From Broken Wings To A Beautiful Butterfly

Sharon Elaine Hodgkinson

It was 2002 and I was a 22-year-old first-time mum bringing up a child with special needs, due to being born at 27 weeks, with the help of my parents. When my daughter was 6 months old, I met what I thought was my Prince Charming here to sweep me off my feet and make everything better.

Things progressed quite quickly for us. We decided to move in together, so we bought our first house. Then we decided to try for our own baby, which believe me was scary because of what I went through with my first pregnancy, and we even decided to get married. Everything seemed perfect and like it was meant to be for us.

When I was 3 months pregnant, we had our wedding. I was all dressed up and looking beautiful waiting to marry the man of my dreams. The wedding was great, we went on to the sit-down meal, and then the evening reception. I wasn't drinking due to being pregnant but still managed to have a good time. My husband made up for the fact I wasn't drinking though with his pints of vodka and red bull (I should have known then and there exactly what I was getting myself into).

I spent the wedding night on my own, well technically I wasn't on my own I had a spider in the bathroom (I'm scared of spiders).

Fast forward to 2005 and we now have 2 gorgeous girls with lots of hospital appointments and stays due to many complications with my firstborn. We seemed to be handling life pretty well, or so I thought. Daily life was always full-on with sorting out my daughter's medical needs and making sure my other daughter had everything she needed. Little did I know that my husband was extremely good at hiding a secret from me; he was actually an alcoholic and life was definitely about to change for all of us in a very big way.

Let me tell you living with an alcoholic is no picnic, it's bloody hard work.

I want you to imagine this image in your head for me. Let's pretend you're me and you're sitting chilling with your kids or trying to do something nice like arts and crafts, and all you can hear in the background is someone constantly shouting your name over and over relentlessly. I bet you're imagining your child when they want mummy's attention when you're busy doing the washing or something. I felt like I had 3 children when he was like this. He would literally want me to stop everything and answer to his every whim no matter if I was busy with the kids, or even trying to get some sleep (God forbid I wanted to sleep).

Most people think that domestic abuse is all about the physical side of things like being punched, kicked, etc. But for most people including myself, the main abuse involves the mental side of things like name-calling. He had several special names just for me; names like bitch, slut, slag, and my all-time absolute favourite (not) cunt. I absolutely hate that word. If I was extra lucky, he would actually call me by my real name but just imagine it in the tone of Ozzy Osborne.

The mental abuse was pretty constant by now and an everyday thing that even though I shouldn't I actually got used to. Sometimes I found myself answering to those names which is crazy.

Don't get me wrong the mental abuse was torture at times and the things he used to say to me were heartbreaking. Remember at the beginning of the chapter I told you that I had a daughter who was born with special needs, well sometimes according to him I only had her so that I could make money out of her. He affectionately called her a cash cow. I mean come on now, can you think of anyone who woke up one morning and thought to themselves that today I'm going to give birth to my first child but not only that make sure she is born prematurely just so that I can make money from her. Whenever he said these mean things, it would break my heart but luckily my daughter didn't really understand what he was saying due to her having special needs.

So, we were together for 12 years and married for 10 and I can honestly say at least 8 of those years were all about the emotional and physical abuse.

I can't tell you how many times the odd people that I did talk to about what was going on would say to me why don't you leave? It's a question that gets asked so many times and usually by people who have never experienced any sort of abuse. Occasionally it would come from someone who has and at the time I couldn't even give them an answer because my brain was so scrambled 24/7. I think what they didn't fully understand is that I wasn't in a situation where I could just up and leave with my children because I would need somewhere with lots of specialised equipment in place for my eldest daughter, so I was literally stuck with nowhere to go and unfortunately nowhere to turn.

You're probably thinking well, what about your family, your parents?

Let me tell you a little about what tends to happen when you are with someone who is controlling, abusive, and a narcissist. They cut you off from the people you love, they convince you that all you need are him and that everyone else would just make things difficult. So, over the 12 years, I sadly cut my parents off so many times. One time in particular lasted about 3 years and believe me, when I was forced to make the phone call telling them that I didn't need them in my life it broke my heart, but I was in a situation where I knew that if I didn't abide by his rules then I would suffer the consequences.

The mental abuse was a daily occurrence now, but now it also included a more physical side. His drinking had literally taken control of him with his favourite being vodka, he loved vodka especially now that I could get a staff discount from where I worked at the time. I would finish my shift and be bombarded with text messages and phone calls to get him a bottle or sometimes he would really splash out and ask for cans of lager. It started off with him wanting a 70cl bottle but that would soon change to a litre bottle and end up with him going to the shop himself later that evening to get more.

Have you ever heard the phrase "she pushed my buttons?' Believe me, I'm still wondering where those buttons are on any man let alone any person in general. He would tell me daily that he only drinks because of me pushing his buttons, I must have been an absolute nightmare to live with.

So let's talk about some of the physical abuse I endured, I would have objects thrown at me and I can still remember the very first time it happened, we were standing in the kitchen and he was calling me the usual names, and because I was too scared to say anything he picked a fridge magnet from the fridge which had very sharp corners and threw it and it hit me on the head. I actually plucked up the courage to ring the police, mainly because the kids were in the house, and when they arrived he literally got a slap on the wrist, he was told not to do it again and to sober up.

This was my very first time dealing with the police and from that moment I felt like I would probably never be listened to. So, the evening carried on as normal and the following morning it was like nothing had even happened, and on we went.

Other objects that were thrown at me over the years included glasses with or without drinks inside funnily enough though they never contained any alcohol well he wouldn't want to waste it now would he, tubs of butter, bottles luckily, they were plastic and never full (lucky me), plates, and of course more fridge magnets.

But the physical abuse didn't stop there he had also begun to attack me with his body. The first time I can remember very clearly, he had been drinking most of the day and as I was coming out of the bathroom he pinned me up against the wall with his hands around my neck, my feet weren't touching the floor and I was struggling to breathe. The only thing that stopped him was my youngest child literally getting in between us both and shouting at daddy to let mummy go, at the time she was only about 6 years old. He eventually let me go and just went back downstairs. I rang his mum once I managed to get my breathing under control and she reluctantly rang the police for me.

The police arrived and he was arrested and taken away

and kept in custody overnight, the officer took my statement and once again I didn't feel any confidence in the police. He was questioned and my statement was apparently read out to him, and his response was well if she said it happened it must have, and he was actually released without charge.

Over the years I was strangled, punched, kicked, slapped, and many objects thrown at me, plus now social services had become fully involved in our lives. We always had them due to my eldest being disabled but now we had full-on involvement with them. Most people would say that they hate social services, I can honestly say I never hated them but over the years when I look back, I was extremely disappointed in them and the way they worked. So, remember I told you that the abuse happened over several years (roughly 8) we had 12 different social workers in that time who all worked in different ways. They would come to the house and introduce themselves and discuss what was going on usually in front of the children. They would sometimes tell us what we need to do but not actually give us any clue on how to accomplish these things or how to get the proper help.

The children were put on a care plan which was absolutely awful. I was made to feel like an absolute failure as a parent by them, and I wanted to scream and shout but I was too afraid and controlled to be able to do that, so I went along with whatever they said to us. They even suggested that his mum who was also an alcoholic was to be left in charge of him whilst I was at work to help look after the children.

My husband did eventually seek help with his drinking and with the help of the GP he was put on medication to wean him off the alcohol. I lost count of how many times he was put on this medication with the occasional success, but it would usually end up with him drinking again and sometimes whilst he was on the medication because I had pushed those damn buttons again.

This cycle went on until November 2011 when I had literally hit that wall that I was sick of banging my head on. I had been at work since 6am that day and on my way home I received a call from his mum saying that she had had enough and had gone home (she lived 4 doors away) I got in to find him passed out on one of the sofas with his pants around his ankles and covered in his own urine. My eldest daughter was sitting in her wheelchair near him watching television and my youngest was upstairs in her bedroom. I made sure that they were both ok and then proceeded to make some tea, he then woke up and off he went to the shop for more vodka, the next few hours were eventful, to say the least. It started with Ozzy making an appearance again, I lost count of how many times he actually shouted my name, my actual name. By this time, I had taken my eldest daughter upstairs and we were trying to chill out in my youngest's bedroom, watching television and doing some arts and crafts.

He proceeded to come upstairs and call me names, jab me in the ribs, and try his best to get a reaction out of me. I eventually went downstairs to get the phone to call the police, but he ripped the phone from my hand and proceeded to kick and punch me repeatedly.

Police were called and for once, I had an officer who actually listened and acted in my best interests.

Fast forward to now. I am abuse free and have used my experiences to help others, I've attended courses to get help for myself, and last year I completed a course to become a level 3 teacher so that I can go out and teach people how to better help and support victims of abuse because I definitely feel there is room for improvement.

My ex-husband passed away in 2019 due to his alcohol issues.

My life has taken a huge leap forward and the future looks a lot brighter. I now have 3 beautiful children who are all unique in their own way and I have met the man I was always meant to be with, and we are currently planning our wedding.

I want to say a huge thank you for reading my chapter and I hope if anything it helps others to seek help and realise that no matter what someone tells you that you are an incredible person/wife/mum and that you can accomplish anything in life.

***

My name is Sharon Elaine Hodgkinson and I'd like to tell you a little bit about me. I'm a full time mum of 3 gorgeous children aged 21, 18 and 7 who are all unique in their own ways. My eldest is disabled and is fully wheelchair bound but has the biggest smile on her face, my middle child is currently transitioning from female to male and I can't even begin to tell you how proud I am, and then we have my youngest who is autistic and keeps me on my toes daily. I'm a domestic abuse survivor and mentor as I feel passionately about helping other women break free from the abuse and change their lives for the better.

http://www.facebook.com/sharonelaine20

Dancing with Desperation: A Tale of Daring to be Different

Rachel Jennings Coudron

In 2015, she looked at me with large saucer eyes astounded by my revelation. In my hand, I carried twenty-four prescribed pills I was preparing to take for the day. Her reaction triggered a cosmic change. As if lightning struck me, I knew I had to change. I had to reclaim my power. I had to take back my life. The next day, I irresponsibly took myself off all the medications I had been prescribed over the previous year (Always consult a physician before making this type of decision... it can be life-threatening). But this is my story, and I was irresponsible. I knew in my gut that if I didn't make a MASSIVE shift, I'd be fifty, taking fifty prescription pills a day. I REFUSED to walk that path. I knew medications didn't lead to more health but more disease and pain. This was the start of my alternative healing journey.

I consulted my aunt, who has a diverse understanding of herbal supplements and vitamins. I explained that I had hypothyroidism, intensive pain in and around my pelvis, and very low energy. She suggested an array of supplements. The next day, I bought them all. I still took more than twenty pills daily, but these were natural. I felt more comfortable. Over the following weeks, I came to a startling conclusion. While I didn't feel magically healed, I realised I felt the same energy and pain levels as I did while on the prescribed medications. This shocked my conventional way of thinking. Wasn't I supposed to feel my best while on the medications? Isn't that what I had been brainwashed to believe? Isn't the core messaging around drugs that, once taken, you can reclaim your life? I came to the life-altering conclusion that the other healing modalities yet to be explored could change the trajectory of my life. After that one conclusion, I became OBSESSED with all things in the holistic sphere.

I devoured every book about toxins, nutrition, alternative care, minerals, supplements, neuroscience, mental health, pain management, etc. I watched dozens and dozens of Netflix documentaries that focused on holistic care. Ultimately, my next action would be to return to the gynaecologist and explain that I was only open to alternative pain management methods. This led me to pelvic floor physical therapy, counseling, journaling, and acupuncture. These modalities, coupled with multiple supplements, orchestrated my recovery. My life has completely shifted trajectories since delving into the holistic universe.

You may think, "She has shared her story from pain to triumph... What more is there?" I wish I could tell you I stayed in that state of healing and power, but life had other plans. The next stage of my journey takes place in a restaurant.

I was giddy with excitement in half of my body and full of dread in the other half. I was about to tell my parents that Thomas and I would move to France. We sat in a booth across from my parents at Cheddar's in Oklahoma in August. My Mom could feel my energy. I exclaimed with glee, "We are moving to France!" Without saying a word, my Mom paused, got up, and left. Later, I unraveled that she returned to her house, which was nearby. In hindsight, I understood her reaction and the time she needed to process the bomb that was dropped on her, but at the time, I was devastated. Why couldn't my Mom be happy for me? It had been my dream since I was a child to live abroad. As time has passed, her true feelings of support and understanding have shown. She now brags to others about how she talks to her granddaughter every day. Unfortunately, these times were not those, and after my Mom walked out, a deep and unabiding stream of guilt settled into my heart. That guilt dug its' talons into my life and would ultimately triple over the next nine months.

Thomas and I could have never imagined that we would discover we were expecting our first child one month later. Our lives were immediately thrown into chaos. Could I leave the only place I had ever known to move to a country where I didn't speak the language and knew only Thomas' family? Could I abandon my innate dreams for my child that centered around growing up as an American? In the end, I decided yes! The call of the wondrous and adventurous heart was strong. I was fulfilling a childhood dream. I saw rainbows and butterflies and did not know of the stormy skies in the background.

I boarded the flight with a sunny and thrilled disposition. I'd uncover it later, but when I disembarked, I was stripped of my autonomy. I was no longer the captain of my own ship.

Language limited my ability to communicate. I could no longer open my bank account, buy my car, defend my values, or build relationships. Vanishing in an instant against my will was my need for connection, love, variety, and contribution. I went from an independent, self-sufficient woman to an utterly codependent woman. My autonomy ended where the comfort level of my husband began. I was contained, and my true feelings were seldom expressed. I lived inside a foreign bubble with no control. My continual sense of feeling like a shadow of my previous self threw me into a depressive state. I felt powerless. I couldn't imagine a future that felt more wholesome or fulfilling. As the guilt of leaving my homeland deepened, so did my depression. I often imagined drowning in the tub or driving into oncoming traffic. I knew I had to change quickly as I wanted desperately to become a mother that nurtured her child. I returned to many modalities I used when recovering from constant physical pain. I took supplements, reconnected with my counselor, started meditating, journaled, and received acupuncture. While these were instrumental in my recovery, my unborn child was the only light inside me. She carried me through the worst days and the overwhelming feeling of isolation. She is the reason that I am still breathing.

She guaranteed a cosmic change. I held onto that sliver of hope. My daughter, Eleonore, arrived on June 19th, 2019. My life would never be the same from the moment she was laid across my chest. Her birth was my rebirth. I found a purpose and a reason to live. I poured my heart and soul into her. I relished those sweet newborn snuggles. I was living the dream. I radiated happiness and felt a high that I've never again experienced. You may be thinking...certainly after my second rodeo with recovering my health... I'd be able to stay on the straight and narrow, but then you'd be wrong. I'd fall far down the cliff only ten months later. I crashed when my love of being a mother became my only defining attribute. I was alone and confused that I'd returned to the same place I'd started. I was still lost. My only identity was Mom. Who was I outside of that parameter? I had not a single clue.

Did I have passions? Goals? Did I have dreams for my life? My previous two health crises prepared me to notice the changes in my body and attitude. I started taking action at the beginning of my depressive feelings to mitigate the intensity of the potential situation. I was motivated to save myself before the worst could occur. When you have experienced depression before and crawled your way back into the light… you'll do everything it takes to not fall back into the black abyss. I poured all of my being into my daughter. I had not a drop left for myself. I lost myself in becoming a mother. After eighteen months of throwing all my energy into my pregnancy or daughter's life, I was only inches closer to discovering who Rachel was in France. Every aspect of my tangible life had changed since moving and becoming a mother. I had no friends, limited support, and only regularly spoke to my parents, husband, and daughter.

My only hope was to reconnect with my passions, which brought me joy and gave me purpose. I recalled moments in my life where I had experienced joy. The memories of being a business owner in the US flooded back. I love the highs and lows of entrepreneurship. Amongst the scare and lockdown associated with Covid, in the summer of 2020, I relaunched my company Coudron's Curiosities. Inside my realm of passion and purpose, I specialise in hand-painted wooden earrings. This decision would be the catalyst to change my entire life. It would propel me to start networking online.

If you have a business, you must interact with people to be successful.

I had no choice. It was either learning to network or admitting defeat. I was too motivated to entertain the idea of defeat. I'd find Hike Those Likes Marketplace and Mums in Business International (MIB) within the online space. When I found MIB, I screeched and hopped in circles with excitement. I had found my people. Mothers who were business owners and understood my struggles. Mothers who were breastfeeding their baby AND running a business. I felt empowered. MIB, coupled with multiple holistic strategies, unveiled a new destination for my life. These modalities were my saving grace. They gave me back my power. MIB was the warm and supportive hug I needed to save myself. Ultimately, I did recover, but my story doesn't stop there. It's been eight years, and I've lived every day without medications.

I can now climb the stairs in my house without pain and train for long-distance running competitions. My physical health has been transformed. I am not the same person I was back in 2015. My jewellery business has grown to international heights. I have shipped to fourteen countries worldwide and made hundreds of sales. In April of 2022, I launched my copywriting business RC Copywriting. I have worked with business owners from five different countries in the last year. The accolades have expanded over the years but have no bearing on my worth. My worth was determined on the day I decided to regain my power and stop taking prescription pills. The day I stopped being a victim. The day I realised change only occurs by taking action. The day I stepped into the sunlight and started to walk the path less traveled. My personal success is not determined by how many products or services I sell but by how many lives I touch and inspire.

My mission for writing this chapter is for you to see I am just like you. Boldly transparent, I've been reduced to less than you on more occasions than I would like to admit. I crawled, scratched, and dragged myself to recovery, and if you are reading this feeling seen for the first time, know that you, too, can create massive shifts in your life. If your heart beats and oxygen fills your lungs, your purpose has yet to be fulfilled entirely. Be bold. Be unapologetic. When your heart shows you the way, follow without hesitation. In May of 2024, I'll do just this. I'll step out of the shadows and into the sunshine and become a beacon of lights to inspire, encourage, and empower men and women from around the globe to reclaim their power and purpose at my holistic seminar. If you are ready to lay claim to your life and re-establish your identity with your needs front and center, join me in France for a life-changing four-day opportunity.

From a heart full of gratitude and love...

Ride fearlessly towards your dreams and jump NOW before you are READY!

With love,

Rachel Coudron

***

My passion for writing can be traced back to my pre-professional days. I spent my high school days writing love poetry, and empowering music. I've been destined to become a writer all my life. Why? I like to capture the essence of a person or brand in words. I love diving deep into your passions, motivation, and purpose.

I am an experienced copywriter, entrepreneur, jewellery designer, social media strategist and most recently an anthropologist who advocates for holistic health modalities. Driven by seeing others succeed, I take pride in providing the best strategies to amplify your social media engagement, increase your confidence, uplevel your health, and grow your pocketbook. As a copywriter, I aim to increase your return on investment and help you expand your business.

Outside the office, I am committed to being 1% better every day. I read books focused on career development, personal development, science-fiction, mystery, and even some romance here and there. I'm fluent in English (and speak medium-level French), which is developing daily as I live in France. I am also a Mother, Wife, and Explorer. You can find me here @rachel.jennings1

Is That All There Is? Perspective And Increasing Gratitude

Jackie McGloughlin

Have you ever had a moment where you ask, "Is that all there is?"

I've had that moment many times in my life – from when I was a small child to now. But how do we deal with this and make our lives better?

Some people advocate looking for the silver linings in the dark clouds. Other people suggest that we adopt a growth mindset. And still others recommend connections to improve things. All of these tips are helpful. I am going to share with you times and experiences when they have transformed my life, and give you prompts to reflect on your experiences.

Silver Linings

When I was just 5 years old, I had an amazing day with my grandmother. I was staying overnight with her and I was so excited because we were going to feed the ducks. Amazing because it was just her and me, and she was always listening (I felt so seen and loved). We got our coats on and headed down the pathway to the duck pond. As we came closer to the pond, I could see that there were no ducks around at all – well, this had never happened before. I was so disappointed and said "is that all there is?" When I looked at my grandmother with tears of disappointment in my eyes, she said "that's okay, I guess they are at another pond today". And we continued walking, she told me a story of how the ducks always come back. As we walked and talked, I held her hand and all was right with the world again. I guess it was never really about the ducks after all. But it was only after I experienced that disappointment, that I realised how special our time was together.

Can you recall a time when you had plans that didn't come through? Maybe it was a cancelled trip, unrealised plans with a friend, or even a movie that ended in a cliffhanger. Given the fact that you are reading this, you have come through that experience. But I invite you to reflect for a moment if there were any small blessings that happened because of the changed plans. For example, did you spend time at home and discover something local that was great? Or maybe you took the trip later and it was amazing?

A wise friend of mine told me that not all days are good, but there is something good in every day. By paying attention to the good bits, we notice them more and more. And as we notice them more, we have an internal shift and can start to bring about more good things in our days. It doesn't mean that we will never have a bad day or a bad moment, but the balance can shift as we change our perspective.

Maybe you've heard this before and you are still waiting

for a change.

There are so many ideas out there about how to live a better life, and some will be a good fit, while others seem like a lost cause. So here I offer you another possibility to address disappointments and the "is that all there is?" experiences in your days.

Growth Mindset

A growth mindset – something my husband mentioned to me years ago after reading something in a book. At the time, I brushed off this suggestion of a growth mindset and continued on my way. For the past few years, I've been doing lots of personal development work and I've been hearing more and more about this concept.

But what really is a growth mindset? We are all born with skills and talents – AND – we can expand these and gain new ones. This often requires hard work, new strategies and help from others, but it is possible. It is something along the lines of learning to tie our shoes when we're very small. We're not born knowing how to tie our shoes, but we can learn this skill when we practice and someone shows us the way. I remember my daughter mastering this skill when she was 3 and she was so excited and so proud! Just like this we can develop skills through practice and help from others. Sometimes though, we forget these things and our expectations need to be realigned.

I remember how true this was when I went to my first Jin Shin Jyutsu class. This was an exciting time because Jin Shin Jyutsu gentle energy treatments I attribute to helping me return to good health from a health crisis. As I was sitting in the classroom, I was excited to receive all the secrets of the universe and how to help myself and others. Well, I opened the first text book – and I was shocked. As I flipped through the book, there were very few words, some diagrams, and lots of empty space. I was so disappointed and asked my friend "Is that all there is?" As the class started, the teacher said' this book is just a starting point. I will share my wisdom and experience, and you will add to it as you study, experience, and practice Jin Shin Jyutsu'. As I delved into the material, I began my journey as a practitioner and came to understand more than I could have perceived at the time. My expectation was for a set of prescribed techniques that would work every time. My expanded perspective is that this is a holistic way of living. My favourite part of this is that we all have the power to heal ourselves even if we need a bit of help from others at times.

Can you recall a time when you were disappointed by a class, teacher, or book? Maybe you were hoping for the magic bullet and realised there wasn't one? Maybe you were hoping for a comprehensive guide to a subject and found more questions than answers? This is an excellent opportunity to grow and experience new things beyond what someone else has set out for you. Did you explore new things that you had not considered before? Was your experience better than you could have imagined with your previous perspective?

CONNECTIONS

If silver linings and a growth mindset are falling short for you, connections may help. These connections can be internal ones as well as external ones. Internal connections are generally about awareness and alignment. External connections include relationships with eternal truths and other people.

Internal connections were difficult for me. 15 years ago I did not have great internal connections or awareness and this led to a major health crisis that forced me to re-evaluate everything. My priority on achievements and monetary compensation was no longer possible. This left a gaping hole and it was time to dig deep and become clear about my values and purpose. While I had been working with my values for a long time, I needed to step it up a bit. I had always had some core values vaguely defined in my mind, but I was still drifting and merely wanting them to be true. So, I got more serious about them and wrote them down. Some key ones are still true for me today: caring, empathy, equity, hope, acceptance, and creativity. These values really came to life when I started intentionally LIVING my values each day.

By living my values, I was more aware and I was able to align my values with my purpose and my actions. For example, I revamped my work goals to explicitly put hope, caring and empathy to the front. Some are easier to do than others, but making progress helps me to continue evolving.

But still, even with this increased awareness and alignment, I was wondering yet again "is that all there is?" Bringing my values into practice was not complete until I improved external connections. My external connections and relationships were still lacking. Each step along this journey had been an evolution that challenged me to my very core – and this phase was no different. These core values were useful, but there was still something lacking. The internal alignment still lacked that connection, contentment, and grounding that I was seeking. I started reaching out and building better connections with other people. This was challenging during the Corona Virus pandemic, but we still found ways to connect – Zoom meetings became commonplace and allowed for connections throughout the world. I found these connections with other people to be the key factor that helped me to gain more satisfaction, more contentment, and vision of limitless potential.

Even with this increased awareness, I still sometimes found myself asking "Is that all there is?" Sometimes things seemed very underwhelming and very arbitrary. For example, sometimes discussions focused intensely on political strife and economic challenges. Of course, it depends on the people having the discussion – some people focused on these things closely, and other people paid little attention to these areas. With these connections, I found myself wondering how things fit into a bigger picture – something more enduring and meaningful.

Around this time, I spent many hours studying philosophy each week. This helped me connect with bigger truths – things that people have been grappling with for centuries. As my connections with the bigger truths (like justice and beauty) strengthened, and I gained a bigger understanding of how I fit into the universe. I have come to realise that each of us must develop our own understanding and beliefs about ourselves and the wider universe. I have heard that people who don't study history are doomed to repeat it. In this case, it's more that I had been drifting without that connection to the bigger picture. These universal concepts, sometimes referred to as universal truths, allowed me to place myself within a broad context and to get clear on my own worldviews – something I'm still developing.

Can you recall a time when you were seeking more value and more alignment in your life? Maybe it was a job that you were showing up to just for the paycheck. Maybe it was spending time and money on things that don't feed your soul. But I invite you to reflect on those times when you have been fully aligned, purposeful and focused on your bigger goals. Is this something that you could shift a small bit at a time? Even taking small steps can add up to big differences over time.

The underlying thread to each of these themes is a shift in perspective and increasing gratitude for your situation and your potential. Seeing the silver linings in experiences helps me to have a broader perspective than the specific concern I have at any given moment. It also helps me to appreciate all experiences and to have more gratitude for the blessings that come on a regular basis. Maintaining a growth mindset, prompts me to try new things even when they are difficult and to have a broader perspective of what is possible. I've been surprised many times that I have great capacity to learn and do difficult things. This isn't something we lose as we grow up, but maybe something we forget to engage with on a regular basis. We don't have to accept our perceived limitations. We can explore new ideas and try things out. Connections have broadened my perspective of who I am and how I fit into the world. Making these connections has shown me that we all have a place in this world, and we all have inherent value.

But you may ask, how does this play out for me? Is that all there is? Being willing to ask what else is possible and to explore it with gratitude for the opportunities and the challenges can make all the difference. When someone asks, would you like to do this? You can jump in and see how it goes. When someone asks, who would like to do x, y or z? You can step forward and expand your experience, your perspective, and your potential. So, what will you say yes to first?

***

Jackie is a gentle, soulful complementary therapist who helps women reconnect with their bodies and empowers them to regain their lives after decades of pain and suffering. She has dedicated her life to Jin Shin Jyutsu after her journey to recovery. When doctors had no answers to her debilitating immune disorder, she boldly turned to complementary healing modalities. Healing her mind, body, soul, and emotions allows her to live an empowered life today. Following her transformation, she opened 'Energy Flows' in February 2020, specialising in Jin Shin Jyutsu (JSJ). Jackie harnesses the innate capabilities of JSJ and most often treats anxiety, depression, auto-immune disorders, chronic pain, tension, stress, and menopause. Over the years, she has honed her skills in intuitively resetting the body's energetic pathways and holds the perfect balance between compassion and functionality. As an intuitive healer, she continues to shatter glass ceilings and preconceived notions about complementary therapy and health recovery journeys. Her success is a testament to her ability to understand her client's perspectives and her unwavering dedication to the lives she changes daily.

https://energyflows.ie/insta-links/

You are good enough, I am good enough

Sarah Ellis

She was sitting on my knee, and she stopped breathing. I tried to save her, but I couldn't – I was not good enough!

This is how my story of not being good enough and how my feelings didn't matter, and that everyone I love leaves me started…at the influential age of thirteen as my eleven-year-old sister stopped breathing in my arms unexpectedly.

You see, I tried with all my might to get her breathing again, it wasn't that I didn't know what I was doing, I had been part of the Red Cross for years and had been trained in life-saving techniques so I should have been able to save her right? The feelings of no this can't be happening, I don't want you to die, you aren't going to leave me, all rushing through my head…but it didn't matter…she died anyway!

The next thing I remember is being told by family members to be strong for my mum and dad as this is going to devastate them…cue my feelings don't matter again, I can't get upset or say anything as it will upset my parents…

and I couldn't save her for them…I wasn't good enough!

This could be seen as a traumatic event, couldn't it? But I did not see it as trauma, I saw it as this was just life, something that happened that I had to get on with, life goes on.

Four years later at the age of seventeen, my parents relocated from the UK to the USA to start a new life and I decided that I was not going to go with them, I was going to stay in the UK. I don't recall any arguing or fighting between us at the time over this decision but ultimately the end result was that they let me stay in the UK. Did I want them to go? No! Should they have dragged me kicking and screaming with them to the USA? Yes! But at the time they felt that they couldn't force me to go, that they were making the right decision by going along with my decision. Guess how this translated into my subconscious… My feelings do not matter, I am not good enough to fight for, and everyone who loves me leaves me.

This could be seen as a traumatic event, couldn't it? But I did not see it as trauma, I saw it as just life, something that happened that I had to get on with, life goes on.

One year later at the tender age of 18, I entered into my first of many abusive relationships, after all, I wasn't good enough for anything else. At 19 I made the decision to have a baby, not in the hopes that it would improve the relationship I was in but because I believed if I had a baby then this was one person who wouldn't leave me, who would love me unconditionally. I remained in this relationship for a few years, always justifying my partner's actions with the usual minimising of the abuse…it is only when he has had a drink, or, it is not physical abuse as he has never hit me only pushed me, pinned me to the wall, had his hands around my throat. My breaking point in this relationship and finding the strength to leave came to a head when I was attacked by him whilst holding my son. This was the catalyst that made something click in my head that I had to leave, not to protect myself but to protect my child. That day, there and then, I walked out the door and never went back. That ended the physical abuse; however, it started a cycle of emotional and mental abuse for a period of time whilst the realisation hit him that I wasn't coming back, that the control was over. At this point, I would regularly have to deal with him kidnapping my child and refusing to hand him back, even though I never stopped any access to our child and never did for the next 18 years.

This could be seen as a traumatic event, couldn't it? But I did not see it as trauma, I saw it as just life, something that happened that I had to get on with, life goes on.

The cycle of entering into abusive relationships of some type continued for the next 5 years. None of these were physically abusive relationships but certainly abusive in other ways, but I felt like I was in control, when I had endured enough emotional and mental abuse I would leave before they could leave me and move on to the next one straight away, I could not be alone, I needed someone, regardless of how they treated me, having someone was better than not having anyone, remember I was not good enough for anything else.

This could be seen as a traumatic event, couldn't it? But I did not see it as trauma, I saw it as just life, something that happened that I had to get on with, life goes on.

When I look back at my career, it follows a very similar theme in some respects. I have always worked in the healthcare industry to different degrees. This career path started when I was just 15 years old when I started working on the weekends at a nursing home. At 15 I had decided that since I no longer had my sister to care for that I was destined to care for others instead, I felt like this was my calling in life, to help others. I progressed in my career over the following years to working on acute psychiatric hospital wards, then to work in the community with people suffering from mental health issues that needed support with their day-to-day living. I felt like I was fulfilling my purpose in life of helping others and it was very satisfying although challenging at times, but I had a focus.

In my late 20's I finally met someone who was not abusive towards me, threw all my eggs in one basket, and uprooted myself and my young child 250 miles away to start a new life as a family together. This relationship lasted 22 years and gave me another beautiful child.

On relocating I switched my career path slightly to start working with substance and alcohol misusing individuals who were also involved in the criminal justice system. Once again, I believed this was my purpose in life, to help others, and this particular group of vulnerable individuals certainly provided me with a focus for my help.

Over the following 12 years, I continued working in this field and my career progressed from starting on the ground level working 1-1 with substance misusers right up to moving into a leadership and management position being responsible for a whole host of staff and hundreds of vulnerable individuals accessing the service. I absolutely loved my management position, but with it came a whole host of challenging issues that I had not accounted for, such as taking care of myself, that thought hadn't even crossed my mind, I wasn't good enough, so now I had this high responsibility, high demanding, high salaried job I needed to go over and above what was expected of me in order to prove I was good enough for such a position. But that's ok, right? Remember, my feelings didn't matter!

Running in the background of my high-stress career, I had issues in my personal life. My son had been diagnosed with ADHD and depression, and this became extremely evident when he started secondary school. They could not deal with his impulsivity and lack of concentration and was labelled the 'naughty kid' and was removed from mainstream school to a pupil referral unit. My son was put in a position of being surrounded by criminal juveniles and 'bad kids' for simply having a mental health diagnosis. Part of him having ADHD was the fact that he was very easily led by peers and did not see risks, so when he hit his teenage years my goodness did he give me a good run for my money. To this day I say to him 'How the heck I didn't end up insane with the antics you put me through is a miracle'. I was regularly having to deal with a distressed child who would consume alcohol and other substances, get in trouble with the police for fighting, and attempt on numerous occasions to end his own life. This was all in an attempt to self-manage his depression and symptoms of ADHD. There was no support offered to him or myself, we were left to just deal with it all ourselves.

I had always suffered with anxiety and depression from a young age, but at this point having to try and manage my son, and my very busy career really started to take its toll on me, and I resorted to medication to help me through and keep my head above water. I vividly remember my boss saying to me 'You are amazing at compartmentalising between your home life and work', both she and I saw this as a fantastic attribute... but if you looked closely it wasn't compartmentalising it was suppressing my emotions and thoughts in order to function on a day to day basis, it was trying to deny to myself that I wasn't coping...and that is ok right? Remember my feelings didn't matter, I wasn't good enough to handle everything successfully.

This could be seen as a traumatic event, couldn't it? But I did not see it as trauma, I saw it as just life, something that happened that I had to get on with, life goes on.

In 2016 my whole world in my eyes came crashing down around me. An incident happened at work that resulted in me having a mental breakdown as a result of work-related stress, forcing me to take redundancy as I was in no fit state to fight the company for my position. In one fell swoop, I had lost my job, my friends, my identity, my health, and my financial security.

I remember literally rocking on the chair in the doctor's office, unable to speak coherently or control my hysterical emotions, blood running from my hands onto the floor as I dug and scratched into my skin with anxiety. I had extremely paranoid thoughts, I was catastrophising future outcomes, having regular nightmares and flashbacks and the help I was offered from the doctor was either a short time in hospital or benzodiazepines to help calm me. From working previously on the hospital wards I knew that this environment would not be conducive to my health, so I took the pills and headed home with a new diagnosis of PTSD, and panic disorder to add to my already anxiety disorder and depression.

This could be seen as a traumatic event, couldn't it? But I did not see it as trauma, I saw it as just life, something that happened that I had to get on with, life goes on.

In the midst of all this chaos, something inside me knew that nobody was coming to save me, that I was responsible for my health improving, and I had to find something or someone that would help me find myself again, so that is exactly what I did!

I started to lean on all my skills and training from my past, it was time to start practising what I had preached for years to everyone I had been working with previously to help them. I started researching other areas I could train in that would help my personal growth and development. Most importantly I found a community of people online who I could immerse myself with and learn from.

I discovered that everything that had negatively happened in my life wasn't just part of life, it was trauma, and I had lots of trauma that I was holding in my body, suppressed in my core, that I hadn't expressed or processed. All the trauma had led to me having the limiting beliefs that I was not good enough, that my feelings didn't matter, and that everyone who loved me left me.

Cue...releasing and processing it all!!!

Was it pretty? Heck no it was very messy and extremely emotional. I had to embrace and integrate parts of my shadow and my inner child in order to become whole.

Was it worth it? Heck yes, I knew that no matter how messy and emotional it got, it could be painful, but it wouldn't kill me.

Did I do it alone? Heck no, yes I admit the majority I researched, learned, and implemented on my own, but I also built up a support network of people to lean on in times of need.

I decided I no longer wanted to enter back into working for others and started my own personal development business, using my 25 years of experience and all the extra knowledge, training, and lived experiences I had gained from the traumas in my life and coming out a better version of myself on the other side to help others. I now have a new, defined, and aligned purpose in life to help women just like myself to live their best life possible and to their fullest potential and I am loving and thriving in life now.

If there is one thing I could say to you from looking back at my life and in hindsight, of all the trauma I experienced it would be to make sure you learn to express and process your emotions, don't suppress them all over and over again or one day it is going to jump up and bite you on the butt!!!!!

No matter what you have been through, know that your trauma or negative experiences are NOT YOU, they don't define who you are, and you can come out the other side a happy, fulfilled, authentic version of YOU.

I am good enough, You are good enough.

My feelings matter, Your feelings matter

Believe it and live it!

Love & Light

Sarah Ellis

***

Sarah Ellis is a mum of 2 boys, and also a Nan to 2 boys! Sarah is a Belief and Mindset Facilitator, Hypnotherapy and Energy Healing Practitioner, and Tarot reader. Sarah has an extensive background of over 25 years' experience working with the most vulnerable groups of individuals in society, and Leadership and Management experience. Her wealth of qualifications, skills, knowledge and personal experiences, is how her business BeWhoYouWantToBecome Coaching and Holistic Therapies was born, and she now devotes her time to helping women who are ready for change to live their best life authentically and to their fullest potential and purpose both personally and professionally. Sarah is known for her no-nonsense approach mixed with a friendly approach and

sense of humour twist.
You can connect with Sarah via:
https://linktr.ee/SJEllis

EPILOGUE

To you, the divine reader, holding this book in your hands at this very moment, please know that our gratitude is truly from the whole heart in having the opportunity to share this book with you. Your presence in joining us and sharing in the journey of "Hear Me Evolve: Voices of the Collective" fills us with deep appreciation.

Thank you for immersing yourself in the depth of 21 chapters filled with what we hope were powerful and inspiring stories. Your support resonates not only with our authors and this book but also extends its touch to lives beyond, reaching survivors through the embrace of Hopefull Handbags.

Your involvement in supporting Hopefull Handbags contributes to the empowerment of those who have transcended domestic abuse. This commitment sets in motion a chain reaction, infusing lives with positive change that reverberates far and wide. For this, our gratitude knows no bounds.

Within these pages, we invite you to recognize that evolution is a continuous journey. Our past and present do not define our future. Each moment presents an opportunity for growth and transformation. You hold the power to write your future, shaping it as you envision.

As you've journeyed through these words, each page carries a message of ongoing evolution, a reminder that happiness and change are within your grasp.

Remember how powerful and strong you are, and together we can be even stronger.

Together we can evolve.

With love and gratitude,

El and Sarah

Printed in Great Britain
by Amazon

29080788R00126